Parish Social Ministry

Cover Design

The cover, *Ite, Missa est*, designed by **Trish Dinkel Crowe**, expresses the Christian community as a pilgrim people in their Eucharistic journey into the world of service and social ministry. *Ita Missa est* is the concluding prayer of the Eucharistic liturgy which commissions the congregation to live out its ministry.

Parish Social Ministry

A Vision and Resource

A Catholic Charities Perspective

Alexandra Peeler

The National Conference
of
Catholic Charities

1346 Connecticut Avenue, N.W.
Washington, D.C. 20036

To parishioners,
who, as the people of God,
are called to conversion
and to a new life
which expresses itself
in service.

Contents

Part I: Visioning It

ONE
Theological Reflections 3

Part II: Doing It
Implementing Parish Social Ministry

Part III: Processes of Social Ministry

NATIONAL CONFERENCE
OF CATHOLIC CHARITIES

1346 Connecticut Ave., N.W., Washington, D.C. 20036 / (202) 785-2757

September 3, 1985

Dear Friends of Parish Social Ministry:

Everyone has a need to be known, and especially, known for his or her best attributes. Even the Lord—"who was like us in all things except sin"—explicitly showed this human quality when he went aside with his closest colleagues, Simon Peter, James and John and asked them: "Who do *they* say I am?" After the apostles repeated what they had heard, Jesus then asked them: "Who do *you* say that I am?"

Organizations have the same need: to know how others—outside the system and those close to it—view them. Organizations also need to reflect and state who they are. This resource attempts to raise identity questions on all three of these levels.

First, how do *they* view the work of Catholic Charities? Who the *they* are is important to us. For some, the important they are often limited to the power figures. For Catholic Charities, the they whose opinion we value must include the poor, the homeless and the hungry, the abused and the abusing, the lonely and the loveless. Who do they say we are? It is my hope that this publication will prompt the widest dialogue about parish social ministry. It can be an opportunity for the they to speak directly or through advocates.

At the second level, this resource reflects a two-year process of people close to the system, those actually involved in parish social ministry. They exchanged their stories, successes, failures, dreams and future plans. This book really carries their story. Like the *Acts of the Apostles*, it is a living history of the work of the Spirit alive with the Church today in the parishes.

x

Finally and most importantly, with this publication the Catholic Charities Movement is itself further revealing its identity. Catholic Charities continues to call itself to be and to become more effectively the presence of Jesus proclaiming: "The Spirit of the Lord is upon me; therefore he has anointed me. He has sent me to bring glad tidings to the poor, to proclaim liberty to captives, recovery of sight to the blind and release to prisoners, to announce a year of favor from the Lord."

With every good blessing and good wish, I am

Sincerely,

Rev. **Thomas Harvey**
Executive Director
National Conference of Catholic Charities

August 27, 1985

Dear Friends:

Following the call of Pope John XXIII for a spirit of aggiornamento in the Church, the National Conference of Catholic Charities in the late sixties began a self-study in the hope of inspiring personal and institutional renewal within the Catholic Charities Movement. A beautiful and challenging statement of the contemporary theological meaning of charity was poetically penned by the gifted and prophetic Msgr. Robert Fox. The call to live the fundamental command to Love is the vocation of every baptized Christian. The social mission of the Church is the responsibility of each Catholic and every parish.

The leadership in Catholic Charities acknowledged that many of our agencies, programs and services were distanced from the life experiences of parishioners. Charities' directors genuinely desired to deepen roots in the life of the Church, to open up opportunities for communication, for participation and for integration of social ministry into the parish mission.

This publication, *Parish Social Ministry*, represents an attempt to capture some of the dynamic efforts made by local churches and Catholic Charities throughout the United States in the last fifteen years. It is offered as a resource to stimulate the creativity and imagination of other dioceses. I suggest that readers seek not so much for models to imitate but for ideas and experiences that will challenge your own conceptualization for a sound integration of social ministry into the life of your parish and diocese.

It is only when we join the active participation of our Catholic people in services, programs and social advocacy with our celebration of worship in Eucharist that we truly witness our following of the compassionate Christ and our belief that in Him we can do all things.

Sincerely yours in Christ,

Most Reverend **Joseph M. Sullivan**

Foreword

This work on parish social ministry from the NCCC should surprise no one. Rather, to me at least, the surprise would be if such a document did not appear. Parish social ministry has deep roots in the Catholic Charities Movement, extending back to the parish work of the St. Vincent de Paul Society in the last century.

More current roots of parish social ministry lie in Catholic Charities' renewal efforts of the early 1970's, in which I had the good fortune to participate.

Three basic thrusts emerged from that renewal: to serve those in need; to humanize society; and to convene others to address the issues of suffering and injustice.

A fundamental underlying tenet of this three-fold function, indeed the very heart of Catholic Charities' renewal, affirms the inclusion of the broader Christian community and all people of good will in the works of justice and charity. The NCCC renewal study, *Toward a Renewed Catholic Charities Movement*, clearly states that "Catholic Charities must be grounded in the participation of the Christian community in the works of charity."

To be "grounded in" denotes a very solid relationship. It is difficult to imagine a relationship much closer than one that is "grounded in." The participation of the Christian community in the works of charity establishes the starting point for Catholic Charities' mission which is nothing less than the social mission of the Church.

Parish social ministry fits exquisitely into the work of Catholic Charities, for the parish represents the Christian community par excellence. It was gratifying to see the emphasis this work places on the participation of all baptized Christians to live out their faith in works of charity and justice. This book firmly establishes Catholic Charities as a major force in advancing social ministry at the parish level.

In the year of its diamond jubilee, how fitting that Catholic Charities' gift to all is this guide to involve the Christian community in the social mission of the Church!

J. Francis Stafford
Bishop of Memphis

Author's Acknowledgments

This book has many contributors. They include both parishioners and social ministry staffs from almost 100 parishes and Catholic Charities agencies throughout the nation. In their small group discussions, the participants reflected upon and carefully structured their vision of parish social ministry. The process genuinely reflected their philosophy of parish social ministry itself, essentially a convening process resulting in action. These convenings were made possible by a grant from an anonymous donor to whom we offer a sincere thank you.

Particular acknowledgment goes to the agency parish social ministry directors who organized the regional parish social ministry convenings and later reported their findings, and whose discussions formed the basis of this work, especially the chapters on principles and integrating parish social ministry into the Catholic Charities agency. This group, which formed the National Conference of Catholic Charities (NCCC) *Parish Social Ministry Task Force*, contributed substantially to the formation of the content. The *Task Force* members included:

Mary Baudouin, New Orleans;
Francis Dolan, Philadelphia;
Shirley Fineran, O.S.F., Chicago;
John Gilmartin, Rockville Centre; NY
Brenda Hermann, MSBT, Alexandria, LA;
Jeanne Orrben, Denver;
Richard Shannon, Manchester, NH;
Carol Sukitz, I.H.M., Pittsburgh;
Mary Zirbes, O.S.F., St. Paul.

A special thank you to **Rosemary Winder Strange** of the National Conference of Catholic Charities who guided the development of this work with enviable insight, good sense, and humor, not only during the regional and national convenings, but also during the writing, editing, and production. As associate director at NCCC in charge of Social Services and Parish Social Ministry, she provided welcome continuity and watchful care to a sometimes unwieldly process. Also, along with her assistant, *Mary Beth Seader*, she tackled the unglamorous administrative details in seeing this project to fruition.

A sincere thank you to *Thomas Harvey*, NCCC executive director, who freely gave enthusiastic support, theological discernment, and editorial advice, and also to the many draft readers in the Charities Movement, especially *Thomas DeStefano*, *Kathleen Walsh*, *Stephen Hay*, *Stephen Gratto*, *Richard Quirk*, *Beth Long*, *Thomas Reese*, *Rolland Smith*, *Elizabeth Apel*, C.D.P., and *Maria Mercedes Hartmann*, S.S.N.D., who offered critical evaluation.

Thanks to the following, who by sharing their experiences, have helped enliven the concepts presented here: *Bob Baker, Donna Butler, Rey Bracamonte, Margaret Cafferty, Gerard Creedon, Peter Della Monica, Mary Ellen Durbin, John Graykoski, David Hougan, Marge Harrak, Tony Lee, Don Leaming-Elmer, Beth Long, Teddie Miller, Jean Mowbray, Tom Myott, Judy Opalach, Rolland Smith, Peter Ujvagi, Josefina Vera,* and *Peter Ward*.

This account of parish social ministry contains a distinct Catholic Charities flavor and perspective, as the impetus and content stem from Catholic Charities agencies. It is Catholic Charities' contribution to the field of parish social ministry.

Our hope is that it becomes a useable instrument for a variety of people who wish to implement or reflect further on the Christian commitment to social ministry.

—*Alexandra Peeler*
NCCC Writing Consultant

Washington, D.C.
September 1985

National Conference of Catholic Charities
Parish Social Ministry Task Force
Convenings

East

Jim Amato, Philadelphia, PA
Maureen Bernard, Haverhill, MA
Antonio Blanco, Brooklyn, NY
Jill Bowen, Peabody, MA
Geoffrey Brahmer, Boston, MA
Jane Caderette, Haverhill, MA
Helene Canberg, Hauppauge, NY
Sr. Gloria Cianci, Bridgeport, CT
Margaret Danner, Harrisburg, CT
Mary Ann Dantuono, Mineola, NY
Thomas DeStefano, Brooklyn, NY
Peter Della Monica, Brooklyn, NY
Denis Demers, Manchester, NH
Patricia Dillon, Philadelphia, PA
Francis Dolan, Philadelphia, PA
Leo Donoghue, Quincy, MA
Arthur Dooling, Bellport, NY
Ruth E. Dwyer, Metuchen, NY
Ann Ferro, Syracuse, NY
Sr. Phyllis Greco, Rockville, MD
Rev. Paul Gregorie, Manchester, NH
Sr. M. Mercedes Hartmann, Baltimore, MD
Sr. Ann Horgan, Syosset, NY
Sr. Julie Kane, Waterville, ME
Sr. Patricia Kelly, Philadelphia, PA
Sr. Joy Kronenberger, Erie, PA

Catherine LaDisa, Lynbrook, NY
Beth Long, Arlington, VA
Julian Miller, Remensburg, NY
Jack O'Connell, Rockville Centre, NY
Sr. Theresa O'Leary, Quincy, MA
Nancy Pierson, Commack, NY
Patricia Quinn, Mineola, NY
Rev. Ed Roberts, Brockton, MA
Sr. Dorothea Ross, Washington, DC
Rosemary Sausen, Wilmington, DE
Sr. Patricia Scarano, Metuchen, NJ
Richard J. Shannon, Manchester, NH
Mary Ellen Sheridan, Philadelphia, PA
Loretta Stepanovich, Harrisburg, PA
Sr. Carol Sukitz, Pittsburgh, PA
Linda Tapler, Rocky Point, NY
Bob Teudesman, Blue Point, NY
Shirley Thomson, Bay Shore, NY
Sr. Mary Waters, Blue Point, NY

Midwest

Julie Barker, Chicago, IL
Nancy Branda, Rockford, IL
Sherry Camden, Chicago, IL
Mary Ann Dubyoski, Cleveland, OH
Mary Ellen Durbin, Lombard, IL
Vera Fina, Maywood, IL
Sr. Shirley Fineran, Chicago, IL
Brian Flannery, Cleveland, OH
Don Gatwood, Indianapolis, IN
Lucille Gutowski, Norridge, IL
Lolande Hennen, St. Paul, MN
Sr. Esther Hofschulte, Lexington, KY
David Hougan, Rockford, IL
Lillian Jones, Indianapolis, IN
Sr. Cathy Katoski, Romeoville, IL
William Kintz, Ft. Wayne, IN
Frank Klein, Chicago, IL
Joe Lauer, Ft. Wayne, IN
Zig Licwinko, Rockford, IL
Vicki Marczynski, Lansing, MI
Tara Markey, Kansas City, KS
Sr. Rita McCabe, Norridge, IL
Mary McClory, Michigan City, IN
Geri McKeown, Chicago, IL
Sherwen Moore, Chicago, IL
Jean Mowbray, Chicago, IL
Tom Myott, Burnsville, MN
Elizabeth Norris, Kansas City, MO
Martha Norris, Warrensburg, MO
Beth O'Donnell, Cleveland, OH
Rita Oster, Chicago, IL
Martha Perrine, Cleveland, OH
Sr. Donna Marie Preston, Chicago, IL
Diana Rivera, Chicago, IL
Maryann Rouse, Omaha, NE
Rev. Tim Sawina, St. Paul, MN
Rev. William Schackmuth, Norridge, IL
Susan Stolfa, Romeoville, IL
Rick Strickland, St. Paul, MN
Sr. Jean Tranel, Rockford, IL

Josephine Vazquez, Chicago, IL
Bill Warriner, Ft. Wayne, IN
June Wilkerson, Chicago, IL
Sr. Mary Zirbes, St. Paul, MN

South

Mary Ann Baudouin, New Orleans, LA
Steve Bogus, Amarillo, TX
Jo Ann Coleman, Houston, TX
Cathy D'Eramo, Houston, TX
Mari Elledge, Fort Worth, TX
Stephen Hay, Lubbock, TX
Sr. Brenda Hermann, Alexandria, LA
Vicki Judice, New Orleans, LA
Sr. Ann McDermott, Ft. Lauderdale, FL
Pat Miller, Ft. Lauderdale, FL
Sr. Miriam Mitchell, Houma, LA
Sr. John Mary Robinson, Montgomery, AL
Dot Shippen, Montgomery, AL
Bill Tierney, Jacksonville, FL
Sr. Kathleen Toland, Augusta, GA
Charmaine R. Williams, Ft. Worth, TX

West

Bill Baird, Denver, CO
Bob Baker, Portland, OR
Nancy Bernatow, Denver, CO
Sue Boucher, Denver, CO
Sr. Georgiana Cahill, Los Angeles, CA
Sr. Jo Chappell, Seattle, WA
Kathleen Connolly, San Francisco, CA
Sr. Kathleen Curtis, Stockton, CA

Sr. Michael Mary Eagan, Denver, CO
Jean East, Denver, CO
Mary Ebner, Denver, CO
Marge Harrak, Oakland, CA
Mary Ann Hillard, Denver, CO
Carolyn Hood, Denver, CO
Sue Kenney, Denver, CO
Gertrude Kinsley, Denver, CO
Suzanne Lanzing, Denver, CO
Sr. Thomas Josephine Lawler, Oakland, CA
Sr. Carolyn Lopez, Tucson, AZ
Frank Maloney, Oakland, CA
Jeanne Orrben, Denver, CO
Edna Pontillo, Denver, CO
Joe Ridgeway, Denver, CO
Al Ruybal, Denver, CO
Joe Young, Denver, CO
Rafael Zambrano, Denver, CO
Sr. Vincent de Paul, Denver, CO

Introduction

American parishes have engaged in social ministry since colonial times. Within the Catholic Charities Movement, parish social ministry has always played an essential role, particularly through the St. Vincent de Paul Society which emphasized lay involvement and parish ministry.

In recent years, the Catholic Charities Movement, through its renewal, has focused more sharply on social ministry in the parishes.

In spite of the increased activity, few major works have appeared on the subject. The NCCC published *National Trends in Parish Social Ministry: A Study of Parish Programs Affiliated With Catholic Charities Agencies* by Sister Mary Vincentia Joseph and Sister Ann Patrick Conrad, almost a decade ago. More recent works connected with Catholic Charities include: *Developing the Parish As a Community of Service* by Loughlan Sofield, S.T. and Brenda Hermann, M.S.B.T.; and *A Parish Social Ministry in the Diocese of Rockville Centre: Parish Outreach,* by John Gilmartin.

Because of the many directions parish social ministry has taken, Catholic Charities' personnel felt a need to solidify concepts, review progress, and explore means to enhance their work.

The NCCC, under a special grant, established a Parish Social Ministry Task Force which convened Catholic Charities' staff and parishioners at four regional meetings to discuss their experiences. From these meetings emerged the need for a resource that would capture Catholic Charities' vision of parish social ministry.

Following the regional convenings, the NCCC Parish Social Ministry Task Force met in May 1984 to distill the concepts gleaned from the regions. The Task Force agreed upon a definition of parish social ministry, identified principles, (which had considerable agreement across the country) and posed questions regarding how Catholic Charities agencies may integrate parish social ministry into their operations. The NCCC also engaged the former editor/writer of *Parish Outreach Review* to participate in this meeting and to later write the resource and "flesh out" concepts with examples.

This is *not* a how-to or a training manual. Rather, the book focuses on a *vision* of parish social ministry and the *processes* involved in implementing it. The 'visioning' of parish social ministry conceptualizes and anticipates the ideal expression of social ministry within the parish community. As a resource, this book offers the experiences of parish social ministry practitioners in the Catholic Charities Movement from around the country who continue to learn and strive toward the ideal.

This book is intended for a wide audience of those who have an interest in parish social ministry: Catholic Charities directors; agency parish social ministry staff; parishioners and parish staff; diocesan agencies; and community groups.

WHAT IS PARISH SOCIAL MINISTRY?

Catholic Charities views parish social ministry as:

the empowerment of the parish as the people of God to fulfill the Church's mission of love, justice, freedom, and peace by communally responding in an organized way to societal and individual human needs.

Empowerment derives from the community's openness to the lavish gifts of the Spirit. Parish social ministry aims to empower people to communion; to love; to human fulfillment; to justice, freedom, and peace— to the Kingdom.

Parish social ministry responds to human needs, whatever they may be, whether hunger, housing, illness, loneliness, employment or fair wages. These needs may affect only one person or one family or they may arise from social policy that pervasively affects many. The response may range from direct service to group action for justice.

Parish social ministry is *organized* and *deliberate*. It is *communal*, belonging to the people, planned and executed by a group. It is not a haphazard, individual response given when convenient.

Consider the components of the concept: parish; social; ministry.

Parish

Catholic Charities views the parish as *inclusive* rather than exclusive, serving *all* who are within its geographical boundaries. The parish community encompasses more than an institutional entity, more than a church building and church membership. The parish is a spiritually-bonded community that *serves*, teaches, and worships.

Social

Essentially social, the parish mission extends beyond the confines of the church doors. The parish links and connects the Church with the neighborhood. Consider the cross atop the Catholic parish, extending vertically, between heaven and earth, and horizontally, across the neighborhood. The parish is the faith community extending, offering itself to *all* those in need in the neighborhood.

Ministry

To minister means to serve, to care, to comfort, to contribute and to utilize our individual gifts for the community. Ministry belongs to everyone, without exception. To each is given one or more gifts for the benefit of the whole community.

Catholic Charities' Role

Parish social ministry may seem like a simple concept—to serve the community through the parish. Yet, in some parishes, social ministry may be difficult to implement or sustain. In others, the concept may be completely foreign. Parish social ministry may not even be accepted as a legitimate, let alone necessary, parish function. Is help available to parishes so that parishioners may fulfill their mandate to serve?

Yes. During their long history of fulfilling the Church's social mission by providing services, calling together people of good will and advocating for a just social order, Catholic Charities agencies gained a wealth of knowledge and expertise which is available to assist parishes in pursuing the social mission of the Church. Catholic Charities and parishes *share* this social ministry mission. In many dioceses Catholic Charities has trained staff to assist parishes to implement social ministry. Not all parishes want or need assistance, but for those that do, Catholic Charities can be an excellent resource.

The question sometimes arises: why is Catholic Charities involved in parish social ministry? The answer comes from Catholic Charities own mission as a church organization: to be of service wherever there is a need, wherever there are people in pain; to work collaboratively with others toward a just social order; and to convene people to discern ways to accomplish charity and justice. "**Catholic Charities must be grounded in the participation of the Christian community in the works of charity**." (*Toward a Renewed Catholic Charities Movement, NCCC, p. 17*).

Catholic Charities recognize the family and the parish as the basic Christian community. The way Catholic Charities serve the community directly relates to the parish. "Catholic Charities and affiliated agencies should function in such a manner that the community at large can recognize them . . . as part of the formal organization of the parish and diocesan Church." (*A Code of Ethics, NCCC, p. 17*).

Part I:

Visioning It

2

Theological Reflections

What is the basis for parish social ministry in scripture, the life and teachings of Jesus, and in Church teachings? Is there a theology of parish social ministry? Why *do* parish social ministry at all? Is there a comprehensive, creative, body of knowledge that seeks to offer a critical understanding of the relationship between the parish and our human condition?

In the course of their routine work, as well as in preparation for this document, Catholic Charities parish social ministry staff and many parishioners from throughout the country discussed and reflected on the theological underpinnings of parish social ministry. Not surprisingly, the many people involved in these discussions and reflections discovered numerous scriptural and Church teaching resources relevant to social ministry within the parish.

Their findings reflect a pattern of four general themes:

- **the dignity of the human person;**

- **the Church's social mission;**

- **each Christian's call to ministry;**

- **and the communion of the people of God.**

These themes constitute the theological basis for parish social ministry and Catholic Charities commitment to social ministry at the parish level.

THE DIGNITY OF THE HUMAN PERSON

This century, which has perhaps not only witnessed but also communicated man's inhumanity to man to an unprecedented degree throughout the world, has also produced profound thinking and highly eloquent statements on the dignity of the human person. Indeed, John Paul II's first encyclical, *Redemptor Hominis*, celebrates that very theme, which has become a mark of his pontificate.

The dignity of the person is rooted in the two most fundamental facts of human history: the first is the loving act of creation, *the creation of the human person in the image and likeness of God*; and the second is the Incarnation, the embodiment of the Son of God within our midst, *to make us all children of God, brothers and sisters*, heirs to the kingdom.

Human Dignity and Creation: In The Image and Likeness of God

God said, "Let us make humankind in our image and likeness. . ." (*Gen. 2:26*).

What is God like?

In the Old Testament Yahweh revealed Himself a little bit at a time. God's very name was unspoken. In each experience with His people, God's image comes more sharply into focus. Yahweh unfolds his image slowly.

In the Exodus, Yahweh reveals Himself as the one who hears the cries of the oppressed; the one who breaks the yoke of slavery; the one who cares for those who are helpless. He entered into a permanent, lasting relationship with His people. He promised that He would be their God, and that His perpetual stance toward them would be one of steadfast love or (in Hebrew) Hesed. God's basic commandment to the people was that they are to be holy, as He is holy, that their lives are to be characterized by steadfast love: Hesed. Actually, that word is much broader than our notion of love. It encompasses justice, respect for the rights of persons, mercy, compassion and affirming, loving kindness. (Jean Mowbray, Chicago, *Theological Reflections*, Mid-west Convening).

The image of Yahweh, then, which He revealed, is one of magnanimous love and faithfulness: our model and potential.

4

Human Dignity and the Incarnation: Children of God

> God so loved the world that He sent His only son. (*John 3:16*).
> We are now God's children. (*I John 3:2*).

With the coming of God's Son into creation, God establishes a new creation, a new order which alters our relationship with the Father. Christ establishes a *new* intimacy between God and God's people: heirs to the kingdom, brothers and sisters of the Son of Man. The image and likeness of God comes more sharply into focus through the Incarnation. God becomes flesh. God's magnanimity breaks forth in its expression—**from Yahweh, the unspoken name, to the Word in human form**.

God's people receive a new *power*—the power of kinship—and through that power a new dignity. "To as many as received Him He gave the power of becoming children of God." (*John 1:12*). With the new power comes new life: "You have been given full life in union with Him." (*Col. 2:9*). The basic, inherent dignity of our humanity has been enhanced by the Incarnation, through which, "God gave human life the dimension that He intended humanity to have from the first beginning. . . . In Christ and through Christ men and women have acquired full awareness of their dignity, of the heights to which they are raised, of the surpassing worth of their own humanity, and of the meaning of their existence." (*Redemptor Hominis*).

The Incarnation establishes a new relationship, a new intimacy, between God and humans and confers upon them the dignity of the Lord.

Social Implications of Human Dignity

The implications of human dignity, renewed in Christ, are awesome. What is our attitude to one another? How do we treat each other? What is a worthy environment for humans? If social and political conditions dehumanize our brothers and sisters in Christ, what do the people of God do to humanize these conditions so that all may develop to the fullest human potential, that is, become more Christic? We are called to participate in divine life by becoming *more fully human*.

In scripture, Jesus notes that human needs require reverent attention:

'Come, you have my Father's blessing; inherit the kingdom prepared for you from the creation of the world. For I was hungry and you gave me food. I was thirsty and you gave me drink. I was a stranger and you welcomed me; naked, and you clothed me. I was ill and you comforted me; in prison, and you came to visit me.'

Jesus also notes all who are in need are deserving of this care.

Then the just will ask Him, 'Lord, when did we see you hungry and feed you or see you thirsty and give you drink? When did we welcome you away from home or clothe you in your nakedness? When did we visit you when you were ill or in prison?'

The king will answer them, 'I assure you as often as you did it for one of my least brothers or sisters, you did it for me.' (*Matthew 25:37*).

Those who have the Father's blessing, heirs to the kingdom, are those who serve the least of His brothers and sisters. **To share in the kingdom of heaven we must share the goods of the earth.**

In recent times Pope John XXIII very eloquently and simply expressed the fundamental conditions necessary to uphold the dignity of the human person. These tenets may be considered the basic standards for human existence throughout the world.

Every person has the right to life, to bodily integrity, and to the means which are necessary and suitable for the proper development of life; these are primarily food, clothing, shelter, rest, medical care, and finally the necessary social services. . . . A human being also has the right to security in cases of sickness, inability to work, widowhood, old age, unemployment, or in any other case in which he is deprived of the means of subsistence through no fault of his own. . . . Every human being has the right to respect for his person, to his good reputation; the right to freedom in searching for truth and in expressing and communicating his opinions, and in pursuit of art . . . to share in the benefits of culture. . . to a basic education and to technical and professional training in keeping with the stage of educational development in the country to which he belongs to honor God . . . to choose freely the state of life which they prefer. . . to establish a family. . . to work. . . to private property, even of productive goods. . . the right of assembly and association . . . to freedom of movement and of residence. . . and when there are just reasons for it, the right to emigrate to other countries and take up residence there. . . to take an active part in public affairs and to contribute one's part to the common good of the citizens. . . to a juridical protection of his rights. (*Pacem in Terris*).

THE CHURCH'S SOCIAL MISSION

Service Implications of Human Dignity

The dignity bestowed on every human through creation and the Incarnation imposes upon the Church her social mission.

The Vatican Council leaders acknowledged this mission when they declared that the task of the Church in the political community is to stand as a *sign and safeguard of the dignity of the person*. (*Gaudeum et Spes*, IV, 76).

The mission of the Church is to safeguard human dignity, which may seem like an abstract ideal. But as Christians, we are intimately bound to our neighbors on many levels. We may ask, "Who is my neighbor?" as the lawyer who wanted to gain eternal life asked Jesus.

Jesus answered with a story that puts the ideal abstraction into very concrete terms. A man traveling from one city to another was mugged, beaten, and left half dead. A priest and then a church official going the same way pass him by. Along comes a person of questionable social standing who administers first aid, takes the man to a hotel for food, rest, and recovery, and then pays his bill.

"Which of these three," Jesus asks, "proved himself neighbor to him who fell among the robbers?"

The lawyer answers: "He who took pity on him."

And Jesus replies: "You, then, go do the same." (*Luke 10:25*).

The lawyer wanted to be holy.

But,

holiness is not a call to escape humanness. It is a call to become more authentically human. Our mission is, therefore, to remove from society all that does dehumanize and, therefore, all that does despiritualize. Seeing Jesus in the other is not a metaphor. In serving others, we are serving them as they are. (Father Austin Walsh, S.T., *Spirituality for Social Ministry*, talk delivered at Catholic Charities Social Ministry Fair, New Orleans, May 7, 1983).

As they are. This key concept of acceptance asks us to remove all the outer trappings that distinguish our lives so we may clearly see the human dignity that underlies and commits us to each other in our relationships. Note the situation of the traveler in Jesus' story: socially and ethnically different, wounded, bloody, unconscious, broke, unaware of who helped him out, and unable to repay. But nothing, absolutely nothing, can detract from the most fundamental fact of the inherent dignity of the person. And who is neighbor?

Again, another lawyer asks Jesus, "What is the greatest commandment?"

Jesus answers: "Love the Lord your God with all your heart, with all your soul, and with all your mind. This is the greatest and the most important commandment. The second most important commandment is like it: Love your neighbor as you love yourself." (*Matthew 22:35*).

One of the last things Jesus did before He left, St. John tells us, was to give His apostles a new commandment: That you love one another. As I have loved you, so you must love one another. (*John 14:34*).

How do you love? This message from Jesus to love one another is frequently linked to the notion of service. **Service characterizes Jesus' actions from the beginning to the end of his public life.**

At the outset He announced in the temple His purpose by reading from Isaiah:

The Spirit of the Lord is upon me
because He has chosen me to bring good news to the poor,
He has sent me to proclaim liberty to the captives
and recovery of sight to the blind,
to set free the oppressed
and announce that the time has come when the Lord will save his people.
(*Luke 4:18*).

In prison, John the Baptist sends his disciples to ask Jesus, "Are you the one John said was going to come, or should we expect someone else?"

Jesus answers: "Go back and tell John what you are hearing and seeing: the blind can see, the lame can walk, those who suffer from dreaded skin diseases are made clean, the deaf hear, the dead are brought back to life, and the Good News is preached to the poor." (*Matthew 11:4*).

Jesus again emphasized the act of service when He washed his disciples feet at the Last Supper.

"When He had washed their feet and put on His clothes again He went back to the table. 'Do you understand,' he said, 'what I have done to you?

You call me Master and Lord, and rightly; so I am. If I, then, the Lord and Master, have washed your feet, you should wash each other's feet. I have given you an example so that you may copy what I have done to you.' '' (*John 13:12*).

The message of love and service permeates the gospels, but perhaps nowhere so dramatically as in the unfathomable actions of the Last Supper.

> As we all know, the Last Supper is the solemn farewell meal that Jesus celebrated with His chosen band . . . . We find Jesus using bread and wine to interpret for His disciples in advance the meaning that His death on the cross would have. He took the bread and wine and said in a sense, this is me, given for you. This is Myself, my Life, which is given that you may have life. And just as the food and drink are consumed in order to sustain the life of the one that eats and drinks, so too, the life of Jesus, the earthly life of Jesus would be given over and ended so that we may come to the fullness of Life. And He says then, "Do this in memory of Me." Could He have meant more than repeating a ritual action? Could He have been inviting all of His followers to give their lives so that others might live more fully? (Mowbray, *op. cit.*).

In recent times, Church teachings have reinforced Jesus' message to love and serve one another, which in a broad sense, defines the social mission of the Church. The Vatican II Documents are explicit:

> Wherever men are to be found who are in want of food and drink, of clothing, housing, medicine, work, education, and means necessary for leading a truly human life, wherever there are men racked by misfortune or illness, men suffering exile or imprisonment, Christian charity should go in search of them and find them out, comfort them with devoted care and give them the helps that will relieve their needs. This obligation binds first and foremost the more affluent individuals and nations. (*Decree on the Apostolate of the Laity*, #8).

The bishops in the United States and throughout the world have reiterated the Church's social mission:

> Action on the behalf of justice and participation in the transformation of the world fully appear to us a constitutive dimension of the preaching of the Gospel, of, in other words, the Church's mission for the redemption of the human race and its liberation from every oppressive situation. (Bishops' Synod, 1971, *Justice in the World*).

The voices of the popes have also emphasized the Church's service mission:

A convinced Christian cannot shut himself up in a comfortable and selfish 'isolationism' when there are rampant the needs and the wretchedness of his brothers. (Pius XII, *Christmas Message*, 1948).

The poor are your brothers and sisters in Christ. You must never be content to leave them just the crumbs from the feast. You must take of your substance, and not just of your abundance, in order to help them. (John Paul II, *Homily at Yankee Stadium*, October 2, 1979).

The message clearly reveals that Christians, those who receive Christ and share in divine life, must act to transform the world and to foster justice in the world. These actions are not add-ons, nice things for Christians to do, or even merely good works. They are essentials, "constitutive." We must take of "our substance," that is, whatever we are and have, to give to those who need, and not offer only leftovers. These actions define our fundamental attitude toward our neighbor and to society, not only as individuals, but as nations, a concept which implies the Christian's duty to political action on behalf of justice. Moreover, in these teachings regarding the Church's social mission, the poor and the oppressed receive our special emphasis and consideration.

EACH CHRISTIAN'S CALL TO MINISTRY

The Church's universal mission to serve all humankind, based on the inherent dignity of the human person renewed in Christ, has a dramatic parallel in each Christian's individualized call to service.

Baptism and confirmation empower all believers to share in some form of ministry. Although the specific form of participation in ministry varies according to the gifts of the Holy Spirit, all who share in this work are united with one another. (U.S. Bishops, *Called and Gifted: Catholic Laity*, 1980).

Through their baptism and confirmation, all are commissioned to that apostolate by the Lord Himself. (*Lumen Gentium*, 33).

These faithful are by baptism made one body with Christ and are established among the people of God. They are in their own way made sharers in the priestly, prophetic, and kingly functions of Christ. (*Lumen Gentium*, 31).

The gifts of the Spirit, cited in scripture, favor us in the sacraments of baptism and confirmation. The baptismal rite inducts the individual into the Christian community and invites the initiate to share the priestly functions, that is, to reconcile all things to Christ. The new member of the community, baptized in the Spirit, is given a new birth by water and the Holy Spirit, who bestows gifts, enabling the newly baptized to share in the intimate life of the Father through the Son.

Likewise, during confirmation, the one confirmed is sealed with the gift of the Holy Spirit. The Spirit empowers those confirmed to transform the world through the community of the Church.

Numerous scriptural sources lend support to the idea of ministry for everyone. St. Paul, in particular had a lot to say about ministry:

. . .each has a special gift from God, one person this gift, another one that gift. (*I Cor 7:7*).

So we are to use our different gifts in accordance with the grace that God has given us. If our gift is to speak God's message, we should do it according to the faith that we have; if it is to serve, we should serve; if it is to teach, we should teach; if it is to encourage others, we should do so. Whoever shares with others should do it generously; whoever has authority should work hard. Whoever shows kindness to others should do it cheerfully. (*Romans 12:6*).

The Spirit's presence is shown in some way in each person for the good of all. (*I Cor 12:7*).

Each one of us has received a special gift in proportion to what Christ has given. (*Eph 4:7*).

Again, Vatican Council II documents declare our obligation to respond to our ministerial gifts:

From the reception of these charism or gifts, including those which are less dramatic, there arise for *each* believer the right and duty to use them in the Church and in the world for the good of human kind and for the upbuilding of the Church. (*Apostolicam Actuositatem*, 3).

Ministry, defined by the gifts of the Spirit, always advances the Church's mission: "for the good of human kind and the upbuilding of the Church." Mission encompasses the Church's broad agenda in the world. Ministry specifies each Christian's role in the scheme of that mission.

The Laity and Social Ministry

In regards to social ministry, it is the laity, primarily, who carry this responsibility. The American bishops and the Vatican leaders recognized and emphasized the laity's role in the Church's social mission to transform all things to Christ through charity and justice.

The laity, by their very vocation, seek the kingdom of God by engaging in temporal affairs and by ordering them according to the plan of God. (*Lumen Gentium*, 31).

Christian service in the world is represented in a pre-eminent way by the laity. . . . Because of lay persons, Christian service or ministry broadly understood includes civic and public activity, response to the imperatives of peace and justice, resolution of social, political and economic conflicts, especially as they influence the poor, oppressed and minorities. (U.S. Bishops, *Called and Gifted: Catholic Laity*, 1980).

Pope John Paul II, especially, has spoken extensively of ministry, particularly the ministry of the laity. In many of his major talks he reiterates the teachings of the Ecumenical Council. Placing special emphasis on the laity's role in politics to advance the causes of human rights and justice, he views their ministry as a vocation, a particular gift and calling which cannot be ignored.

The Second Vatican Council rightly emphasized that the primary task of the Catholic laity is to impregnate and transform the whole fabric of human social living with the values of the Gospel. (John Paul II, *The Important Roles of the Laity*, Nov. 4, 1983).

Is it not the laity who are called, by reason of their vocation in the Church, to make their contribution in the political and economic dimensions, and to be effectively present in the safeguarding and advancement of human rights? (John Paul II, *Opening Address at Celam*, January 28, 1979).

It is their specific vocation and mission to express the Gospel in their lives and thereby to insert the Gospel as a leaven into the reality of the world in which they live and work. The great forces which shape the world—politics, the mass media, science, technology, culture, education, industry and work— are precisely the areas where lay people are especially competent to exercise their mission. (*Papal Talk at Limerick*, Ireland, October 1, 1979).

I also see the Catholic laity open to the field of politics in which there are often most delicate decisions to be made affecting problems of life, of education, of economics, and therefore, of the dignity and rights of man, of justice, and of peaceful social living in coexistence. (John Paul II, *The Important Roles of the Laity*).

15

Through the laity, the Church relates to the social-political realm. In that arena, the laity access the political process to transform the social order toward peace and justice and radicalize the world toward its Creator, the Word become flesh. Here the people of God assume their role as a priestly people, a people who, through their gifts from the Spirit, *mediate* between heaven and earth, and *reconcile* all things to Christ.

The laity's call to ministry is not to be taken lightly.

We are gifted, not for ourselves, but for others. We are called to use our gifts *for others*. Although each person's gifts are particularized, programmed as it were for each individual, the end result of the application of the gift is for the good of the *community*.

The Model for God's people beckons them to be faithful to this gift and call.

No Christian is exempt from his evangelical responsibility. No one can be substituted for in the demands of the personal apostolate. Every lay person has a field of apostolate in his personal experience. . . .We are responsible for a gift that has to be transmitted faithfully. (John Paul II, *The Important Roles of the Laity*, 8, 4).

The gifts of the laity tend the great forces which shape the world. Lay ministry essentially equals social ministry. Contemporary Church teaching emphasizes the laity's role in social ministry.

We have spoken of the dignity of the human person, and of mission and ministry as theological underpinnings of parish social ministry. How then are these related to the parish?

COMMUNION OF THE PEOPLE OF GOD

A fourth theme which emerged throughout the NCCC theological discussions focuses on communion—communion in the sense of community, unity, people of God, solidarity. Again, scripture and Church documents offer a solid basis for understanding the notion of community, the unifying effect which lies at the heart and direction of parish social ministry.

We look first to what is Church.

According to Vatican II, "the Church is a sign of intimate union with God, and of the unity of all mankind. She is also an instrument for achievement of such union and unity." (*Lumen Gentium*, 1).

The Church then is a symbol, an indication of God's union with His people, as well as a means, a tool, a device for achieving unity among all people.

". . . the Church shines forth as 'people made one with the unity of the Father, the Son, and the Holy Spirit.' The mystery of the holy Church is manifest in her very foundation, for the Lord Jesus inaugurated her by preaching the good news, that is, the coming of God's kingdom. . . . The Church receives the mission to proclaim and to establish among all peoples the kindgom of Christ and of God." (*Lumen Gentium*, 4, 5).

The images of the Church as described in Lumen Gentium and rooted in scripture, are manifold: the Church is a sheepfold, a flock, a tract of land to be cultivated, the edifice of God, the household of God, the holy temple, the Holy City, our Mother, the spotless spouse, the Mystical Body, the Bride of Christ, the people of God. In these images, the element of community stands out (flock, household, people); an aspect of structure appears prominent (edifice, city, temple); intimacy receives emphasis (bride, spouse, mother); and an element of incompletion—anticipation, becoming—(awaiting cultivation) is noted. These characteristics of the Church unfold a mysterious, structured, intimate community moving toward the kingdom and participating in Divine Life.

The image of Church as a people of God, however, dominates the identity of the Church in modern times. Vatican II stressed this image, rooted in the Old Testament, above all others.

Eighty-one times in the Old Testament, the people of Israel are referred to as Kahal Yahweh, or the people of God. When they were a helpless slave people in Egypt; when they stood at Sinai and received the covenant, the commandments; and when they returned from Babylon and restored the temple, they were the Kahal Jahweh, the people of God. And when the prophets spoke in judgment because the widow and the orphan were not cared for, it was not individuals or only isolated leaders who were scolded and subjected to their judgment; rather, it was the people as a whole. "Are you, my people, faithful to the covenant?" was the question of the prophets. (Thomas Harvey, "Maintaining Catholic Identity in a Pluralistic Society: Some Reflections," *Hospital Progress*, p. 50, January 1983).

About 250 B.C., he writes, during the time of Jewish settlements in Greece, Rome and the Mediterranean basin, Jewish religious leaders sought for words in the pagan cultures that would convey their values and identity. "They struggled to find words that would capture the meaning of the people of God. They could find no religious term that would adequately convey its sense." One of the words they adopted was ek-klesia, meaning "those who are called out," which in Greek culture referred to the assembly of all the people in the city-states who were called out to make decisions about the common good.

> The root of this word appears in the adjective ecclesial, "pertaining to the Church." From the translation, one discovers the deep consciousness of the Jewish religious heritage as to who the Jews were: a people with a tremendous sense of community and responsibility, called out by God to accomplish the common good. Here the bishops of Vatican II located the primary focus of the Church's consciousness of its own identity in the modern world. (Harvey, *op. cit.*, p. 51).

Yet the Jews' identification as *the* people of God had no triumphalistic meaning attached to it, he adds. Chosenness was not based on *merit* so much as on *mission*.

Father Harvey relates another concept—*priestly* people—to the people of God and the mission of the Church. The term priest, in its more formal rendering is pontiff, or high priest, rooted in the Latin word pontifex, meaning "one who builds a bridge."

18

"The concept involves mediation and reconciliation, values desperately needed by the common good of society today—values of a priestly people. . . .The world needs a 'priestly people' who view themselves as *chosen to bring about the common good*, which is seen as the will of God. The world needs this Church."

Again, Father Harvey relates the concept of the people of God to the mission of the Church.

God says that Israel would be His people by acting as God Himself acted— that is, by caring for the widow and the orphan, the weak and neglected. Jesus will echo this in the New Covenant when He says, 'This is my commandment. Love one another as I have loved you.' A rational and human logic of love would have settled for 'as I have loved you, so you must love me!' Jesus did not leave the Church any such easy love poetry. In starkly clear terms He said: feed the hungry, shelter the homeless, give drink to the thirsty, heal the sick, be merciful, blessed are the persecuted, and so on. He talked about a world of sight for the blind, and liberty for captives.

The Lord did not give these directives to the Church because they are nice or poetic. Indeed they constitute the fabric of what the Church is. They must be our action plan. (Thomas Harvey, "The Church: Called to Serve," *Charities USA*, March 1983).

The Church's mission, as noted previously, is to spread the Good News, the Gospel, and the Gospel values. Paramount in the Gospel values is the concept of human dignity. If the Church is to remain faithful to her mission, she will reach out to those whose dignity is compromised.

"If the Church makes herself present in the defense of or in advancement of man, she does so in line with her mission. . . . **Her evangelizing mission has as an essential part action for justice and the tasks of the advancement of humanity**." (John Paul II, *Opening Address at Celam*).

IMPLICATIONS OF MISSION, MINISTRY AND COMMUNION

For the Parish

For most Catholics, the Church experience takes place at the level of the parish community. The mission of the parish and of the Church coincide. The parish community is summoned as the people of God. As Bishop Joseph Sullivan stated, "The parish . . . is there to *convert* people to become a community of people who have compassion. It ought to be a place where people come together and are challenged by the experiences of participating in that life. . . . The hope which social ministry in the parish opens up is an evangelization, the opportunity to be converted or tested to the roots and depth of their value system." ("Parish Outreach: most hopeful sign in Charities," *Parish Outreach Review*, No. 16, p. 3).

The parish, as the Church, aims to develop an intimate, structured community moving toward participation in Divine Life. It, too, signifies unity of all people. The parish mission is to proclaim the establishment of the kingdom, and the Good News of the Gospel, to evangelize. **Essential elements of that task include action for justice and service to human needs**.

Parishioners are to be doers, and not hearers only. The Spirit summons their response. Their amen means to live out their lives according to the Gospel values. As members of the Eucharisitic community, **as a priestly people**, they answer the call to ministry, according to their gifts to serve and to give of themselves, as Christ does in the Eucharist. And **they are called in *community*, not as individuals, but as Church**.

These last points—*called in community as a priestly people*—provide the rationale for social ministry at the parish level. The reflections at the Denver convenings offer us some insights into the notion that **Christians are called not only individually, but in community to fulfill their ministry**.

Parish social ministry then is not just a vehicle to permit action by the believing individual, but a means to permit the whole Church to enter into the process of Redemption, a process which continually re-energizes the Church and all of its structures. Moreover, parish social ministry incarnates this responsibility within the framework of the principle of subsidiarity: participation and implemention of the highest ideals of the Gospel within those structures nearest the life of believing people. (*Denver Parish Social Ministry Convening*).

The parish, no less than the Church itself, must practice the mandate of Jesus to serve one another. "The issue really is people have got to see the Church as a *servant* Church. They have to see the Church as a witness to what it is about, and they have got to see that manifested in their lives, the corporate life of the parish community," explains Bishop Sullivan. (Sullivan, *op. cit.*).

For Catholic Charities

There sometimes remains a slight hitch between the call and the doing. Pope John XXIII in *Mater et Magistra* offers a very significant insight in this regard. "Consequently, it is not enough for people to be instructed according to the teachings of the Church on their obligation to act in Christian manner in economic and social affairs. **They must also be shown ways in which they can properly fulfill their duty in this regard**."

"**Shown *ways* in which they can properly fulfill their duty**." Herein lies the basis for a structured parish social ministry and for Catholic Charities involvement in parish social ministry. Effective ministry demands knowledge and methodology. Parish social ministry, precisely because it is structured and based on proven methodologies, provides parishioners the means and ways.

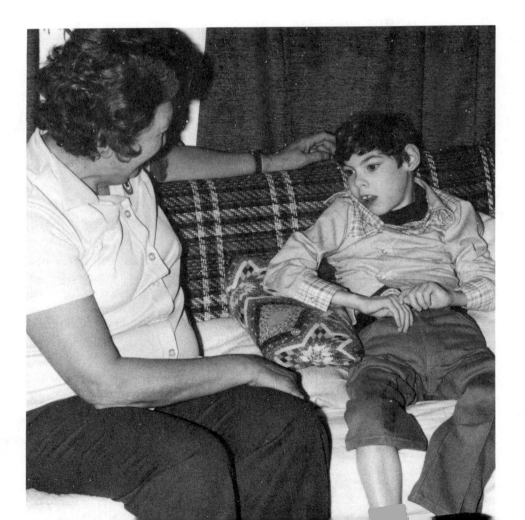

"We have a competency within Catholic Charities. We never ought to lose that competency whether it's a skill in organizing, providing consultation, doing good personnel work, management, counseling, clinical work, setting up homes for the retarded or programs for the sick, or organizing people around social justice issues," Bishop Sullivan says.

Catholic Charities, because it has the skilled personnel to provide training regarding means and methods, acts as a *partner* to the parish in the local diocese for bringing parish social ministry to fruition.

The National Conference of Catholic Charities, in its policy and mission statements and in its renewal efforts, places substantial emphasis on parish social ministry as part of its own mission.

Catholic Charities views social ministry at the parish level as "the embodiment of the Servant Church at the local level. . . .Genuine social ministry stems from the reflection on the experience of parishioners, as they attempt to express and discover their faith through their own experiences and those of their neighbors." (*Policy Statement on Parish/ Community Social Ministry*, 1978, NCCC).

Similar sentiments were expressed in the Council's Decree on the Apostolate of the Laity: "The laity should accustom themselves to working in the parish in close union with their priests, bringing to the church community their own and the world's problems. . . .all of which should be examined and resolved by common deliberation." (*Apostolicam Actuositatem*, 10).

What is the role of Catholic Charities in parish social ministry? The NCCC mission statement declares:

the social mission of the Church is the foundation and reason for being of Catholic Charities . . . .While the obligation of charity is universal to all the 'people of God,' Catholic Charities agencies are entrusted by the local diocese with special responsibility for carrying out this mission for those activities and services that require an institutional rather than an individualized approach. Agencies of Catholic Charities are commissioned in a special way to confront the scandal of human suffering.

To fulfill this responsibility, the mission of Catholic Charities necessarily involves actions of service, advocacy, and convening. (*Code of Ethics*, pp. 11, 12).

The special responsibility and *commissioned in a special way* mean that Catholic Charities have resources, skills, knowledge and experience to undertake social ministry in *cooperation with the parish*. The experience and skills of many Catholic Charities staff make Catholic Charities uniquely suitable to offer parishes the special training, guidance, and resources needed to undertake social ministry. Catholic Charities, in its role as convener, also acts as enabler, facilitator, and catalyst. In fulfilling its own mission, *Catholic Charities commits itself to the participation of the Christian community in the ministry of charity and justice.*

24   *The Homeless*

TWO

Principles of Parish Social Ministry

Practitioners of parish social ministry in the Catholic Charities Movement have surfaced a set of principles, or standards, which form the basis of Catholic Charities parish social ministry. These principles, distilled from the regional convenings by the NCCC Task Force, stem from Catholic Charities practices and reflections. The principles act as operative guides in the development of parish social ministry. **Parish efforts which envelop all these principles realize the ideal expression of parish social ministry**.

Although many agencies and parishes, as in any new thrust, strive to reach this ideal, few have as yet achieved it completely. Most parish social ministry efforts fluctuate along the continuum toward the ideal. Parish social ministry is a creative process. "It's expression is a dynamic and changing art of the agency or parish," says Sister Shirley Fineran.

A summary of the principles follows. The first four receive highest priority, for they constitute the essence of parish social ministry, without which, any parish social ministry effort remains less than authentic from a Catholic Charities perspective.

1. **Parish social ministry builds community.**

2. **Parish social ministry nurtures and intensifies the Christian's baptismal call to ministry by reflecting on lived experience in light of the Gospel values.**

3. **Parish social ministry empowers the parish to:**
   discern Gospel values,
   exercise these values in the community and
   develop lay leadership.

4. **Parish social ministry addresses social and community needs through direct service and action for justice.**

These first four principles set the norm which validates parish social ministry. The next set of principles relate to and flow from these first principles. They point more distinctly to *the manner* in which parish social ministry is expressed.

5. **Parish social ministry recognizes and respects the distinct gifts, needs, resources and diversity of the local geographical and diocesan areas.**

6. **Parish social ministry transcends parochial and provincial issues and limitations by bonding with other groups, parishes, churches, organizations, agencies, and all people of good will.**

7. **Parish social ministry fosters a preferential option for the poor.**

The NCCC Parish Social Ministry Task Force hopes to see these principles applied in all parish social ministry efforts. However, the development of people challenges even those most skilled, and in practice, any parish social ministry effort may emphasize one or more of these principles and overlook others. By examining these standards, those engaged in parish social ministry may increase their understanding and measure their progress.

BUILDING COMMUNITY

Parish social ministry builds community.

One of the main tenets of parish social ministry declares that it builds community. Some view community-building, or developing the people of God, as the prime function of parish social ministry.

"The primary goal of parish social ministry is uniting men and women with God and with each other," claims Thomas DeStefano, executive director of Brooklyn Catholic Charities. It is "an effort aimed at the development of a people. Parish social ministry exists in the fullest sense when it is a process that brings people together in a consistent and meaningful way; when it develops an awareness and an understanding of the problems and the oneness of the human condition; when scripture, prayer, and celebration are a part of developing awareness and where action and services grow out of that awareness."

However, of all the principles discussed here, the community-building aspect poses the greatest challenge. Numerous roadblocks to community-building exist in the practical, day-to-day world.

"The hard part is building the relationships among people. Once that is done, the tasks come easier," admits Judy Opalach, who works in Catholic Charities diocesan parish social ministry office in Cleveland.

Parishioners must constantly question their values in terms of the Gospel. Establishing relationships with others from different economic, social, racial or ethnic groups sometimes proves difficult even within the same parish, not to mention neighboring parishes, other religious groups, or community groups. Barriers such as fear, prejudice, or selfishness break down slowly. But "by addressing common problems together and by working through common projects, barriers are broken and reconciliation takes place," observes Jeanne Orrben, former parish social ministry director, Denver Catholic Charities. Parish social ministry confronts these barriers by converting that energy, through the power of the Spirit, into works of charity and justice.

In instances where these barriers obviously exist, some parishes attempt to overcome them by holding healing services, such as those carried out in a cluster of inner city parishes in Cleveland. "We attempt to go beyond the hurts," says Ms. Opalach. The question she asks is: "How, as Church are we different?"

The community-building aspect of parish social ministry is rooted in the theological concept of the people of God. The process for effecting the servant Church is a corporate and communal one. Community provides the framework for services. Parishioners attest to their unity at the Eucharist celebration and acknowledge themselves as the people of God—the Church, and the Communion of Saints—in the Creed at liturgy. But the reality of community does not end at the altar as much as it begins there. "Community is discovered in our common struggles and pain," says Father John Gilmartin, Rockville Centre diocesan director of Parish Outreach. But we also celebrate our oneness when we celebrate our struggle at the Eucharist liturgy, he adds.

Parish social ministry, while strengthening the bonding of one to another as brothers and sisters in Christ, creates a powerful sense of community.

Community, as Evelyn Whitehead points out in *The Parish In Community and Ministry*, may be both *primary*, as in families and other intimate groups, or *secondary*, as in social organizations, such as when a number of people find they share a concern of some significant aspect of their lives.

Both types of community-building occur during the parish social ministry process. At the outset of the process, during the meetings of small groups, a strong, emotional sense of community develops. When the parish joins with other parishes on a diocesan-wide action, or with a number of community organizations to accomplish a similar goal, the secondary community bond develops. This natural bonding strengthens the faith community. Moreover, especially today in our mobile and fast-paced technological society, creating a sense of community takes on added meaning by filling the void of natural communities previously available in the extended family, clan, or neighborhood.

Building Community: Brooklyn

Catholic Charities in the Brooklyn Diocese directs much of its staff effort to developing community. Basically, Charities acts as enabler, assisting parishes to develop a core group of volunteers who in turn engage other parishioners, who then, fortified with Gospel values, resolve to humanize unacceptable conditions that impair members of the community.

Developing people and building community starts slowly and demands substantial energy and time in order to establish trust and comfortable relationships among all those engaged in the process.

Immaculate Conception parish, located in a working class, low and moderate income neighborhood in Queens, initiated parish social ministry in the early 1980's. The pastor, who had been familiar with Catholic Charities efforts over the years, invited Charities to help establish social ministry in the parish. The pastor identified several parish leaders as a core group who would link other parishioners into the process.

"In the early stages, we met a few hours a week with the pastor and the core group," said Peter Della Monica, Charities' regional director for Community Development. Charities listened to their concerns and helped lay the foundation of social ministry. Core members recruited other parishioners. "We conducted formalized training with this first tier of social ministers," explained Mr. Della Monica. Parishioners discussed Gospel values, theology, leadership development, management principles, and ways to do needs assessments.

The social ministers set out to identify community needs, beginning with an open convening. Small groups with a facilitator for each group, identified broader community needs. The frail, home-bound elderly received the highest priority and they were targeted as the parish's first concern. The parish established a Human Service Center as a focal point for its social ministry. General information and referral services, linked to Catholic Charities, and other services were developed. The social ministers also tapped, as another resource, the Eucharistic ministers who visited the elderly on communion calls. The Eucharistic ministers were asked to observe and report to the social ministers any unsuitable living conditions among the home-bound elderly.

Some social ministers from Immaculate Conception attended Community Board meetings (a mechanism set up by the City to discuss public issues such as land use, municipal services, etc.). "The social ministers from Immaculate Conception brought striking statistics to the attention of the Community Board," said Mr. Della Monica. "They described what was going on behind the doors of the home-bound elderly—no services, no means for shopping, inadequate information about their benefits." The social ministers brought a Gospel perspective to these meetings and through their input helped increase services to the home-bound elderly.

Another vital aspect of the parish social ministry effort concentrated on involving the frail elderly themselves in social ministry and on their participation in the parish community celebrations. "Many of the elderly are now tied into the network of care through telephone reassurance to

help others. They call two or three people on their list each morning to see how they're doing, then report back to the parish," explained Mr. Della Monica. "The social ministers have also taken 10 to 15 of the elderly into the group to meet the caring system and to celebrate," he added.

"Through the sharings of work done, reflections, liturgies, and social meetings, a sense of community is created," he said. The building of community continues to evolve as extended families and others participate in and celebrate parish social ministry.

CALL TO MINISTRY

Parish social ministry nurtures and intensifies the Christian's baptismal call to ministry by reflecting on lived experience in light of the Gospel values.

As was shown in the theological reflections, all are called to ministry, all are gifted for ministry. Ministry is the obligation of every baptized person. It is not a choice. Parish social ministry helps parishioners' discover their gifts and provides the means through which they respond to their call to ministry.

The nurturing aspect of parish social ministry involves knowledge and methodology. As Pope John XXIII stated, **the people of God must be "shown ways in which they can properly fulfill their duty**." One of the methods used by Catholic Charities in nurturing parishioners to discover their gifts includes reflection on the Gospel and the life experiences of the parishioners.

The experiences of the parishioners determine the concrete starting point upon which the reflective process begins. What constitute the experiences, the reactions to success and failure, good fortune and bad, to pain and disappointment? What conditions affront their dignity and that of their neighbors? What Gospel passages relate to these experiences? What values does the Gospel offer and how do they correspond to those of the people?

A process of gift discernment helps acknowledge the gifts of the Spirit within the parish community. Group process effectively uncovers the

31

community's gifts and assists parishioners to identify their own gifts. Also, the group process recognizes that the gifts belong to the community and not solely for the individual endowed with them. The gifts are to be used; each person is accountable.

An element of renewal also characterizes the group process as new people join and others leave. Through this ongoing renewal, the parish social ministry process recognizes that the gifts of the parish and the individuals may change.

Ministry embodies a missionary element; that is, as parishioners are commissioned or sent in their ministry to act on their call, they in turn call others to ministry. "The call to ministry also leads to greater ecumenical contacts with other churches and faiths," adds Father Gilmartin. "In fact, this might be one of the clear signs of greater unity among people—of God uniting us—at the level of human need."

The **parish social ministry** process **offers a structure** for discerning the gifts of the community, **for reflecting** on the Gospel values and the life experiences of the community, **for planning and organizing the implementation of the gifts** for the community, **for mutual support, and for celebrating** the gifts of the community.

Emphasizing the Baptismal Call to Serve: Alexandria-Shreveport

Emphasis on the baptismal call to service has been one of the hallmarks of Catholic Community Services of Alexandria-Shreveport.

Sacred Heart parish, on the Red River in Pineville, La, which has 800 families, exemplifies this principle. When Msgr. Henry Beckers became pastor in 1982, he recognized the many activities in the parish, but that only a few people staffed them. Msgr. Beckers, firmly believing that the baptismal responsibility belonged to all, contacted Catholic Community Services to discuss his concerns and with their help, he embarked on a parish-wide campaign to stress the baptismal call to service. "Catholic Charities trained the parish council and worked with the committees that were overseeing the programmatic aspects," said Sister Brenda Hermann, M.S.B.T., Catholic Community Services diocesan director.

Msgr. Beckers first conducted an educational campaign regarding the baptismal call through his homilies and the parish bulletin. He then encouraged the parish council to begin a renewal process focusing on their role in helping the parish implement the mission of Christ and the Church. The parish council conducted a needs assessment, held a series of open meetings, and created a parish pastoral plan.

The parish council and the pastor also instituted a family dinner on Wednesday evenings prior to religious instruction, which drew from 150 to 400 parishioners. "Parenting classes were held simultaneously with the religious instruction for children. This plan flowed from the belief that adults need to continue to develop in their faith if ministry is to continue," explained Sister Hermann.

The parishioners responded by forming a Service Club to meet immediate needs in the community, many of which included those in nursing homes, a state mental institution, and a correctional institute for women, all of which were within the parish boundaries. The parish council coordinates parish social ministry activities, but the parishioners are responsible for the service. Recently, the parishioners began one-to-one service ministry.

"The people's call to ministry is continually reinforced. We continue to meet with the parish over social concerns," Sister Hermann said. "While there may be times of discouragement, the stress is always that the people carry out the mission of Christ, a responsibility of baptism."

EMPOWERING THE PARISH

Parish social ministry empowers the parish.

Empowering the parish to act in its own behalf as a local expression of the people of God, reflects another key goal of parish social ministry. Empowering parishioners means to bring to fruition their decisions regarding social and community needs. To empower is to put into action the potential which the Spirit brings.

The principle of empowerment embodies self-determination. The parishioners determine needs and how to meet them through a process of reflection, consultation, assessment, planning, action, and evaluation.

Another corollary to the principle of empowerment, concerns ownership. Parish social ministry belongs to the people of the parish. They determine the needs of their community and they decide on the ways to meet these needs.

Catholic Charities emphasizes that parish social ministry belongs to the whole parish. Catholic Charities and other consultants act as resources to the parish by offering an effective process, skills training, and advice to assist the parishioners in their ministry. But the parishioners do social ministry.

As social ministry belongs to all the parishioners, no one person or group in or out of the parish can corner the social ministry market. All are called.

All are gifted, too. The third aspect of empowerment embraces the concept of leadership. Parish leadership, which requires recognition and training, comes to the fore in many ways throughout the entire social ministry process. During each segment of the process, various aspects of leadership develop. Some may lead during the time of reflections; others may be consultants; some lead while assessing; others in the planning and action; and some lead during the evaluation. Leadership assumes high visibility especially during times of action, which demands constancy, courage, discipline, and the ability to lead others to cling to the goal before them.

"Situations do exist in which parishes provide services, but empowerment is clearly not operative," observes Kathleen Walsh, director of Catholic Charities, Lubbock, Texas, in cautioning practitioners to an awareness of a limited view of service ministry.

The principle of empowerment calls for expanding that opportunity to minister to *all* parishioners so they may also offer their gifts to the community. A situation in which parish staff members assume responsibility for social ministry by personally attending to social needs does not necessarily constitute parish social ministry. If such were the case, the parish would merely remain an outpost for social service; and although that activity certainly is worthwhile, it does not reflect an authentic parish social ministry.

The concept of empowerment sometimes remains a stumbling block to agency staff who have been trained to act directly as service providers. However, many agencies, including those in Denver, Chicago, Oakland, Arlington, Cleveland, Hawaii, and elsewhere, are making outstanding strides in overcoming that tendency by adopting the role of catalyst, consultant, and organizer.

Empowering the Parish: Portland, Oregon

Portland Catholic Charities provides a good example of an agency that fosters empowering parishioners in their call to ministry. The agency acts as a technical resource to parishes by facilitating the group process. Through this process the parish:

- conducts its own needs assessment;

- surfaces priorities;

- develops a consensus on ways to meet its needs;

- initiates programs;

- implements programs.

In this process, emphasis focuses on leadership development, parish participation and developing relationships among parishioners and others outside the parish.

"Catholic Charities doesn't offer a program," states Bob Baker, executive director. "The parish, enabled and empowered, is the decision-maker."

The facilitating process, however, is slow. In two years, 12 out of 122 parishes in the diocese started parish social ministry. To reach more parishes, Charities now focuses on clustering, or linking groups of parishes either geographically or with diocesan programs such as Birthright. In one instance, upper/middle income suburban parishes surfaced a need for pastoral counseling, determined a need for a pastoral center, and a way to support it. In another instance, 9 inner city parishes joined with 10 interdenominational churches to act on common concerns. Catholic Charities assisted the organization with its financial development.

The Portland experience exemplifies the principle of empowering the parish to discern needs and to act on Gospel values in meeting those needs. **Ownership, self-determination, and leadership development feature prominently** in these parish social ministry efforts.

SERVICE AND ACTION FOR JUSTICE

Parish social ministry addresses social and community needs through direct services and action for justice.

This principle illustrates the *dual* nature of the activities of parish social ministry: service and action for justice. The underlying theological principle indicates that the parish is an integral part of the broader community, the neighborhood, city, and state and that it helps to meet the needs of that community.

Both service *and* action for justice are necessary and legitimate expressions of parish social ministry. Service, on the one hand, responds directly to an immediate need. Service acknowledges the immediate situation of the recipient and the giver. It takes people where they are. A family's house burns down. The parish community provides shelter, food, clothing, and sees to their emotional needs. An elderly person needs transportation to the doctor. A shut-in needs visitors. A widow needs emotional support. Opportunities such as these abound in any parish community. And parishioners can be organized to provide many one-to-one, as well as self-help group services.

Action for justice, however, requires a different approach. Action may grow out of service experiences, which raise awareness to issues broader than the immediate needs. Many elderly in the community may need transportation to the doctor, or to shopping, or recreation. Group action, including members of the parish and other groups and organizations, can accomplish what one individual alone cannot do. Pressure may stimulate a public or government agency to provide community transportation service for all the elderly who need it. Or the group may establish such a service through their joint resources.

Action for justice can also transcend local issues. Some issues, such as nuclear war or the unborn child's right to life, reflect universal concerns. Here again, action for justice challenges various levels of society, including the political realm. Action for justice implies an understanding and knowledge of the social and political system which creates the negative condition.

Action for justice is frequently a long-term process that offers little immediate satisfaction, but it provides a valid and necessary dimension of parish social ministry.

Both types of activity—direct service and action—require knowledge, skills, and planning. These must be developed and fostered. Catholic Charities parish social ministry staff frequently provide training so that parishioners can develop the skills to perform social ministry effectively.

Meeting Community Needs
Through Service and Action: Chicago

Catholic Charities parish social ministry in Chicago has worked with about 100 parishes in addressing community needs through direct services and action. One urgent community need which engaged parishes in both service and action concerned the issue of hunger. Charities assisted parishes by conducting educational workshops to increase the parishes' awareness of hunger in their community and by helping them to assess the need.

The parishes' response to this community need, explained Sister Shirley Fineran, director of the agency's parish social ministry, consisted of developing food pantries, legislative advocacy in the form of letters to legislators asking for increases in food stamps, and special prayers.

"The parishes became aware that there was a need for more than giving out food," Sister Fineran said. Some became involved with coalitions such as Bread for the World, the Illinois Coalition Against Reagan Economics (ICARE) and the Food Research and Action Center (FRAC).

The agency also organized and coalesced its efforts to fight hunger in the community through a Food Development Program. The agency offered supportive services, organizational assistance, and/or food assistance to parishes involved in legislative action, food pantries and food cooperatives.

At the service level, Charities trained parish volunteers to set up food pantries, how to do intake and follow-up, and generally provide a high level of service. The agency also sponsored a food distribution center that provided quality, fresh food to those in need at a quarter of the commercial cost by utilizing parish volunteers, pooling buying power, and eliminating profit. Charities also networked affluent and poorer parishes so that resources could be shared.

The action for justice centered on advocating for two food bills in the Illinois legislature, and increasing the public's awareness of hunger. The agency held news conferences about hunger at parishes, conducted news conferences in conjunction with the city's mayor, and hosted a visit of the Physicians' Task Force on Hunger in America to publicize agency and parish efforts.

Catholic Charities was also a major force in creating a network of city and state agencies to work on the hunger issue. The agency developed services on a city-wide basis to train volunteers and staff at neighborhood food pantries and provided coordination of emergency food programs so that services fit the needs of the hungry in different communities across the city.

The Chicago example illustrates the parish/agency partnership and the value of networking and coalition-building in meeting community needs through service and action for justice.

RESPECTS DISTINCTIONS

Parish social ministry recognizes and respects the distinct gifts, needs, resources and diversity of the local geographical and diocesan areas.

Each parish community has its own distinct needs and responds to those needs with its particular gifts. Parish social ministry fosters the recognition of diverse parish communities and their distinct ministries within the diocese. It is important to address the unique needs of each parish and discern the unique gifts and resources of the parish. Acknowledging differences and distinctions serves as the starting point to respecting gifts.

The question then becomes, how to discern the parish's needs, gifts, and resources. Here again, the parish may consult with others who have the necessary skills to assess needs and discern gifts. Frequently, Catholic Charities parish social ministry staff can offer assistance to the parish in providing a variety of options for needs assessment and train parishioners to undertake the needs assessment themselves. Catholic Charities staff, or other experienced organizations (such as Ministries Center for the Laity), can also provide direction for the process of discerning leadership and gifts within the parish. According to Jeanne Orrben, Catholic Charities can assist in an analysis of the parish, its ethnic makeup,

income levels, attitudes on issues, functions of existing groups and committees in the parish, and relationships between the pastor, staff, and parishioners, etc.

Respecting Community Distinctions: Lubbock, Texas

The Catholic Charities agency of the new diocese of Lubbock places considerable emphasis on the distinct needs and gifts of its parishioners, 80 percent of whom are Hispanic. Sharing resources receives high priority as most parishes do not have sufficient resources to undertake independent activities. In one parish social ministry endeavor, three parishes joined with local Protestant churches to share the expenses and work of sponsoring a refugee family from El Salvador. Two parish social ministry committees provided housing, food, and clothing for a mother, father and three children who stayed in Lubbock for several months while awaiting permanent visas in Canada. This project received monetary assistance from a third parish community.

Twinning of resources proved successful in another part of the diocese, O'Donnell, Texas, where St. Pius X parish coupled its social ministry with Campaign for Human Development (CHD) funding. The parish applied for and received a local CHD grant to retrain seasonal farmworkers. The parish used the grant to establish a ceramic coopertive project. It bought molds and ceramic materials and obtained volunteer instructors to teach the farmworkers to make and sell their ceramic goods.

In Lubbock, the distinct needs and gifts of the community determine the character of parish social ministry.

TRANSCENDS PAROCHIAL ISSUES

Parish social ministry transcends parochial and provincial issues and limitations by bonding with other groups, parishes, churches, organizations, agencies—with all people of good will.

Closely related to the principle of respecting the diversity of the local diocesan community, is the principle that proposes that no one parish community can do everything by itself. The parish may be limited in its resources or particular gifts, but within the diocese there exist other parishes, churches, organizations, agencies, or individuals with whom the parish can cooperate for the good of the community. Particular issues in the wider community may arise in which the parish does not share a particular need, but nonetheless may contribute resources and gifts that are helpful to others. In such a case, the parish extends a cooperative spirit by sharing itself.

This principle also helps guarantee that the parish will not stay bound to its parochial views, but will open itself to growth through its association with others. As **no one parish is representative of the universal Church**, the parish benefits by opening itself to others. A deep respect for the diversity and integrity of other groups characterizes such openness. Such openness, however, expresses one of the most difficult attitudes to achieve in parish social ministry. Effective cooperation may require a unifying catalyst. Catholic Charities parish social ministry staff often possess the interpersonal skills and knowledge of techniques, such as networking, and coalition-building to achieve inter-parish and parish/community joint action.

Expanding the Parish Vision
Through Networking: Cleveland

The Parish Safety Network in East Cleveland involves five inner city parishes that banded together to address the issue of neighborhood and personal safety. In 1982 Bishop James Lyke convened urban parishes as a means for the parishes to discern their needs. Crime and safety emerged as a prime issue concerning many parishioners in East Cleveland. A subsequent analysis by Catholic Charities re-confirmed that finding as an ongoing concern. Charities Parish Social Ministry Office collaborated with various diocesan groups including the Commission on Catholic Community Action and Catholic Youth Organizations, to draw on available resources to assist the East Cleveland parishes to address their concern.

The bishop requested Father Gallagher, the vicar for East Cleveland to convene the pastors from the six parishes in the area and determine if they would work together in a pilot project on the safety issue. Five of the pastors enthusiastically agreed.

At the same time, Charities Parish Social Ministry staff were aware of a community organization in the area that was also addressing the safety issue. "We saw it as a means for the parishes to plug into. Although it was a small area with many parishes, we found that the parishes didn't communicate with each other," said Judy Opalach of the Parish Social Ministry Office which became instrumental in opening communication lines among the parishes as well as with the existing community organization.

"We convened parishioners and key leaders from the six parishes to talk about their fears, what they wanted to address, what had already been done, and what was successful," she said. After that meeting, Parish Social Ministry convened representatives from the five parishes that joined the Network: St. Philip Neri, St. Thomas Aquinas, St. Casimir, St. Vitus, and St. George, in addition to St. Mary's Seminary which was located in the neighborhood. Charities provided technical assistance to the Network which planned, conducted, and chaired the inter-parish meetings.

The first problem to overcome centered on apathy and creating trust among the racially and ethnically-mixed parishes. Parish Social Ministry helped direct the parishes to consider the issues underlying crime and safety, and to ask the question, "How are we, as Church, different? What are we as Church about in the neighborhood?" The issues of healing, forgiveness, and trust developed and continue to receive attention, along with the safety issue, Ms. Opalach explained.

The small core committee proposed three objectives for the parish network to address: home and personal safety; children and teen safety; and improved police response to calls for help. The core committee then convened the Safety Network parishes to discuss the objectives.

At this large convening, parishioners broke into small working committees relating to one of the three objectives. Some of the working committees moved to join with the neighborhood community organization and work on police response time and the possibility of establishing a 911 emergency number. Parents with school children joined with the school committee to conduct a safety campaign focusing on precautionary measures, and a fingerprinting program. One group is considering inviting other denominations to join the Network efforts. The Holy Name Society from one parish took special interest in the safety issue and extended invitations to the Holy Name Societies from the other parishes to join them in their efforts.

Catholic Charities Parish Social Ministry workers foster the Network's progress by re-convening pastors so they may continue to encourage their parishioners and by helping to plan a healing service at another convening.

The Cleveland example illustrates both the value and difficulties in overcoming parochial limitations by bonding with others. Although overcoming group fears has been difficult and initial parishioner response was less than ideal, Ms. Opalach believes the Network is making progress, and most importantly it is developing a "sense of community."

FOCUS ON THE POOR

Parish social ministry fosters a preferential option for the poor.

Jesus was poor. During His lifetime He gave special emphasis to the poor and the marginal people of society. He associated with known sinners, outcasts, and despised tax collectors. He saw their giftedness and to some He entrusted His mission. He healed lepers, the lame, and the blind. To the poor, he preached the good news. Are His followers to do less?

As Jesus' own example and the Gospels remain the source for the direction of ministry, parish social ministry must also emphasize the gifts and needs of the poor. The parish, in its evangelization efforts, must include as an essential part, action for justice and a commitment to the poor. Although all needs in the community are valid, to be true to the spirit of the Gospel, the needs of the poor receive priority.

NCCC's *Code of Ethics* is clear on this point in describing the mission of the Catholic Charities agency:

> It has a further responsibility in promoting and conducting programs of assistance and service to address the needs of people in all socio-economic groups, but *to have special concern for the neediest and most vulnerable*, to serve as their advocate where this is necessary and to help them to develop the capacity to become their own advocates. (p. 12)

Parish social ministry makes a definite preference for the poor.

Examples of parish social ministry may include material assistance such as food banks and clothing shops. It may also involve assisting the marginally employed by encouraging baby-sitting coops., respites for homebound mothers, or aid in home health. Sometimes what is needed are actions for justice, perhaps to help obtain shelter for the homeless or improve health care benefits.

In the parish social ministry process, special care must be taken so that the poor participate, not only as recipients, but as partners in determining the means to address their needs. "...while Charities must speak out for the poor, the more desirable goal is to enable and assist the poor to speak out for themselves." (*Toward a Renewed Catholic Charities Movement*, p. 32).

Though frequently in need of some material assistance, a poor person

44

is rich in other ways and has something to share. Since parish is inclusive, the parish social ministry process must also encourage each to share what they uniquely have to share.

Focus on the Poor: Philadelphia

Philadelphia Catholic Social Services Parish Social Ministry places particular emphasis on the poor. "The nature of our parish social ministry is dictated by the nature of our parishes—urban, poor, and mostly minority," explained Francis Dolan, director of Parish Social Ministry. Thirty seven (of 306) parishes in the archdiocese are doing parish social ministry and 30 of these are in poor, minority neighborhoods.

"Meeting the needs of the local communities varies; there are 37 different ways. Where there is an active parish council, they have a direct voice. In others there may be less community voice in how social ministry takes shape. But all are overwhelmed by the needs of the community," Mr. Dolan said. "**The community perceives the parish as a center for assistance**."

At Most Blessed Sacrament in West Philadelphia one of the striking community needs included day care service in a neighborhood where many working mothers could not afford existing services. "The parish developed a day care center, resulting from an assessment of the community. The need was clear that many single parents were without day care." The day care center, located in parish facilities is run at cost by the parish.

At St. Agatha/St. James parish, the need for clothing was significant and the parish developed a thrift store. It hired community people to run the store which receives donated clothing from all over the community.

Another parish, Transfiguration of Our Lord, mobilized the community around the issue of vacant houses. They researched and found that several vacant houses were bought by one person and they are now pursuing the implications of this development for the community.

The Philadelphia parishes' option for the poor may be born of necessity, but the parishes and the agency demonstrate their commitment for this option through the hiring of social ministry staff for each participating parish. (Those parishes that can, pay the full cost. For others, the diocese subsidizes the cost).

Philadelphia has one of the largest parish social ministry staffs and virtually all work in poor parish communities.

"All the pastors are committed to parish social ministry—some more than others. But they really want to help the folks who knock on their door for material assistance," Mr. Dolan said.

The agency has begun to place more emphasis on the community's participation in developing social ministry at the parish by fostering the development of parish volunteers, several of whom have been hired as parish social ministers. "We try to involve parishioners. It's more visible in some parishes than in others," Mr. Dolan stated.

The Philadelphia experience also shows that **the pressing demands of assisting the poor materially often overwhelm other efforts.** "It's a struggle," said Mr. Dolan. "All the parishes have some volunteer effort, but it doesn't always sustain itself. The worker gets bogged down with the amount of work and the number of people knocking at the door. How to meet their needs by drawing more on each other is a challenge."

CONCLUSION

These examples show the principles of parish social ministry in practice: the development of a strong relationship among people; careful preparation of people for their ministry; empowering people to self-determination; addressing community needs through direct service and action for justice; respecting the distinct needs and gifts of the community; building relationships among groups outside the parochial environment; and determined efforts to serve the poor and to involve them in services.

The principles characterize an ideal expression of parish social ministry. But parish social ministry essentially remains a process of bringing people together, in awareness of their mission as a unified people, so they may heal the pain of suffering and advance an environment worthy of their humanity.

THREE

Integrating Parish Social Ministry Within the Catholic Charities Agency

In the early 1970's, a number of Catholic Charities agencies embarked on a new journey toward a broader and deeper social mission. The heart of this mission centered on involving people in the social mission of the Church. The emphasis in Charities' service delivery shifted from a firmed-up program and preconceived ideas about meeting social needs, to one of listening and finding the real concerns of the community. The parish moved to center stage as the arena for both discerning and responding to community needs.

These developments led to deeper questions about Catholic Charities' relationship to the parish, prompting agencies to reconsider their mission and to reexamine their basic structure.

What is Catholic Charities' role in developing parish social ministry? Do Catholic Charities agencies have an essential relationship with parish social ministry? How do the agencies initiate and develop parish social ministry? How does the agency integrate parish social ministry into its structure?

The NCCC Parish Social Ministry Task Force in their discussions viewed parish social ministry as much more than an agency program. It considers **parish social ministry a direction for the agency, a primary function of the agency, a developmental, on-going process which should permeate agency activity**.

Such a view may seem radical to some, but this view has considerable support in NCCC documents and policy statements. The basis for this view rests on the interpretation of Catholic Charities' role within the life of the Church and the relationship between the parish and Catholic Charities.

CATHOLIC CHARITIES' MISSION AND THE PARISH

Catholic Charities exist to fulfill the social mission of the Church. The preamble of the National Conference of Catholic Charities' Cadre report of the early 1970's recognized Charities' affinity with the total Church: **"Catholic Charities must be grounded in the participation of the Christian community in the works of charity."** (*Toward a Renewed Catholic Charities Movement*, p. 17).

Furthermore, in its statement of intent, the report beckons Charities to **"assist the Church and the Churches to respond more vigorously to the Christian message of love and justice through action."** (*Ibid*, 29).

Catholic Charities' mission statement reiterates Charities' purpose, goals, tasks and activities as consonant with the social mission of the Church (*Ibid*, 11), and for most people, "Church is best understood as existing in parish/neighborhood communities; therefore Charities works for people in parish/neighborhood communities." (*Midwest Regional Parish Social Ministry Convening*, April 1984).

The continuum of the Church's social mission extends from the local parish to the universal Church. Catholic Charities, whose own special mission is to foster the social mission of the Church, plays an important part in linking the local parish and the broader Church in that mission.

Charities had recognized this relationship between the agency and the parish communities in its renewal study of the early 1970's. "Particular consideration should be given to relationships with parishes. . . ."(*Toward a Renewed Catholic Charities Movement*, p. 35).

Clearly, in their renewal efforts, **Catholic Charities saw their role as essential in assisting the parishes to both live out the social mission of the Church and to more fully inculcate Gospel values**.

"Our mission statement says we have to involve the local community in discerning needs and developing responses. We have to be about service, but the way we deliver service is by working closely with the parishes in discerning human needs and appropriate responses," said Thomas DeStefano, executive director of Brooklyn Catholic Charities.

The agency's first step toward integration is to relate parish social ministry to the agency mission.

More recently, the NCCC Statement of Mission views Charities and parishes as intimately bound to each other. The parish/agency relationship aims toward more than mutual support and close interaction, actually toward structural links through parish representation in the agency's program and policy decisions. In fact, the NCCC mission statement denotes the relationship between the agency and Catholic Charities as an organic one, for it sees the parish playing a vital role within the agency structure: **"In the case of diocesan Catholic Charities, the members of the local parishes should be included through *significant* representation on all groups which determine policy and program."** (*A Code of Ethics*, p. 13).

Denver Catholic Community Services illustrates this directive to a significant degree.

When first established as a department within the agency in 1971, parish social ministry emphasized education and social action. In 1974, the agency shifted its focus to greater parishioner involvement. According to Jim Mauck, executive director, the parishes still saw Catholic Charities as having the major responsibility for service ministry within the Church. "Social ministry wasn't integrated into the parish structure; it was an add-on," he said. Nor was parish social ministry fully integrated into the agency.

One of the ways in which the agency increased the parishes' role more intensely involved the agency's board of directors. Parishioners sit on advisory boards that elect representatives to the board of directors. In effect, the parish representatives became the board of Catholic Community Services, with parishes setting Charities' policies to a substantial degree. With regard to further integration of parish social ministry, the agency, Denver Catholic Community Services, utilizes long-range planning to develop a mission statement, goals, and programs that implement the parish's thrust in all agency services.

The relationship, then, between Charities and the parish is primary. **The parish is a key means through which Charities fulfills its mission**. The parish may choose to ignore Charities (unfortunate, perhaps) but **Charities cannot ignore the parish**.

INTEGRATING PARISH SOCIAL MINISTRY WITHIN THE AGENCY

How does the agency integrate the concept of parish social ministry into its structure in practical terms? In most cases, integration is a matter of degree. During the early years of Charities' renewal, a number of agencies decentralized their services. Soon afterward, parish social ministry came into prominence and several agencies incorporated this concept into their decentralization efforts. Brooklyn Catholic Charities exemplified this move toward decentralization and incorporated parish social ministry into its operations.

"The traditional service model of the Church had been to provide an already designed service package, rather than to talk to the community

about its needs and assist it in working out its own problems. We changed the traditional concept of Catholic Charities," said Thomas DeStefano.

"We tried to expand the concept of ministry to include service at the parish level," said Sister Mary Rose McGeady, D.C., a former director of one of the Brooklyn Charities diocesan vicariates. "We had to learn the parish system and to relate service within the context of the parish. It took us a while to learn. At first we weren't speaking within their experience. We were coming in with our own agenda. Now we listen."

However, in some cases, agencies utilized parishes primarily as a delivery system for agency services. Unless the principles described earlier apply, then decentralizing agency services and housing them on parish property does not necessarily constitute parish social ministry. Using the parish as a means to deliver services does not indicate that the agency has integrated the concept of parish social ministry into its structure.

The key questions remain: Was developing the parish community as the people of God an agency goal? Did Charities nurture the parishioners' baptismal call to serve? To what extent did the agency empower the parish to determine and implement the services being offered?

EXAMPLES OF AGENCIES RESTRUCTURING TO INTEGRATE PARISH SOCIAL MINISTRY

The following examples describe the experiences of several agencies which restructured with the intent to more fully integrate parish social ministry into the agency's operations. Some may exemplify the principles of parish social ministry to a greater extent than others, but each illustrates common concerns encountered while achieving a measure of success.

Parish Social Ministry Teams in Each Vicariate: Honolulu

Catholic Charities of the Diocese of Honolulu is among the most recent agencies to restructure utilizing parish social ministry as the major agency focus. A study by the diocesan Bishop's Special Committee for Catholic Social Ministries completed in early 1985 recommended a new and central role for parishes. (*Study of and General Plan for the Social Ministries of the Catholic Church in Hawaii*, Diocese of Honolulu, February 1985).

> In the restructuring, parishes will become the primary centers for social ministry. They, in turn, will be assisted by their vicariate and a member of the Parish Social Ministry Team, Multiple Resource Agencies, and the Office for Social Ministry and Catholic Charities. (*Ibid.*, p. 14. See accompanying chart in Appendix, page 00).

Much of the support for developing social ministry within the parishes will come from the new parish social ministry teams, one for each of the seven vicariates in the diocese.

> The parish is the primary base for the community service and action of the Church. Central to this restructuring, therefore, is a Parish Social Ministry Team which consists of professional parish/community organizers, with at least one for each vicariate.
> These organizers will work with the vicars to assist each parish to develop its own unique process and program of social ministry. The organizer will work at the invitation of the parish leadership, will analyze the situation of the parish internally and externally, will assist the parish to undertake an assessment of needs and possible activities, and will assist in the linking of parishes, especially their volunteers to the resource agencies. (*Ibid.*, pp. 14–16).

The former Parish Outreach Program (of the now defunct Catholic Social Service agency) has been incorporated into the Parish Social Ministry Teams.

According to Catholic Charities diocesan director, Rolland Smith, "The center of our plan is based on the parish. Catholic Charities is an agency of and for the Church. The key is to have a coordinator in every one of the seven vicariates. Each vicariate has a cluster of parishes."

Another key element aims at developing the parish as community. The vision of the parish as offered in the diocesan *Plan for Social Ministries* expects the parish community to:

- reach out to each other to identify their concerns and resources;

- act together in concert to form new institutions and change old ones in order to meet the needs of people throughout the community;

- express their concerns and celebrate their victories in liturgy;

- reflect on the Gospel values which motivate them;

- cooperate with other organizations in the Church and with other community groups; and

- assume responsibility for the parish. (*Ibid.*, p. 10).

The role of Catholic Charities includes coordinating the Parish Social Ministry teams and the various professional resource agencies, such as Catholic Services to Families, Catholic Service to the Elderly, and the Catholic Immigration Center, each of which has its own director and board. In addition, Catholic Charities Office for Social Ministry oversees Criminal Justice Ministry, St. Vincent dePaul, Catholic Committee for the Handicapped, CHD, and the Justice and Peace Commission. (See organizational chart in Appendix, page 00).

Another vital aspect of the restructuring concerns the role of the bishop. The study group recommended that the bishop communicate to the priests, religious and laity that:

- social ministry is essential to our Catholic faith and a characteristic of a renewing Church;

- each vicariate is to develop a social ministry plan and every parish is to develop its social ministry; and

- the Office for Social Ministry will assist vicariates and parishes in moving towards these ends.

The Honolulu parish social ministry effort embraces many of the major principles discussed in the previous chapter. Prominently emphasized in the restructure plan are the Church's social mission and the building of community; empowering the parishes; transcending parochial limitations by bonding with other parishes and agencies; respecting the distinct gifts and resources of the local communities; addressing social and community needs through services and action for justice; and optional preference for the poor.

The enthusiastic and wholehearted support of the bishop and the diocesan agency director will encourage the development of parish social ministry throughout the diocese. Social ministry may rightfully gain its essential and prominent place in parish life. Hopefully, parish social ministry will permeate the life of the Church in the Diocese of Honolulu.

The reorganization in this diocese has come at a fortunate time, enjoying a number of advantages, such as the collective experience and emphasis on parish social ministry which the Catholic Charities Movement has espoused for more than a decade. The Honolulu study team, in the absence of a diocesan mission statement, also consulted the NCCC *Code of Ethics* for guidance regarding Catholic Charities' mission. These supports, along with a diocesan Charities director who has many years experience in developing parish social ministry, provide a solid foundation for the new direction of social ministries in the diocese.

Partnership with Parishes: Rockville Centre, Long Island, N.Y.

Rockville Centre was among the early innovators in making parish social ministry a major thrust of the agency. It provides the perspective of an agency that restructured through decentralization more than a decade ago.

According to Rev. John Gilmartin, director of Rockville Centre's Parish Outreach, the agency began decentralization in 1973 by establishing a regional office, called a Community Life Center, that offered multi-services. At the same time, three parishes established pilot outreach centers.

As decentralization developed throughout the diocese, the agency established seven Community Life Centers, headed by regional administrators, with each Center servicing about 20 parishes. The Centers offer individual and family counseling, mental health, geriatric, and youth services as well as training, support and supervision of the parishes' service ministry coordinators. The regional administrators convene the coordinators in their region on a monthly basis to discuss needs, identify issues and plan appropriate responses.

In addition, the Centers employ liaison workers to assist the parishes in their parish social ministry efforts. The liaison meets weekly with a coordinator from the parish to review procedures, select core workers from the parish, review cases, and facilitate relationships with other social service agencies.

According to Father Gilmartin, parish social ministry focuses on three primary functions:

- to convene the Christian community to identify its social needs, and to act to serve those needs;

- to serve the needs of the suffering community; and

- to advocate with and on behalf of those who suffer from unjust social systems.

The concept of partnership between agency and parish characterizes Rockville Centre's parish social ministry endeavors. "As partners, the parish community and Catholic Charities join to continually enliven charity and justice within the human community as a concrete response to the gospel message to 'love and serve one another.'" (Rev. John D. Gilmartin, *A Parish Social Ministry in the Diocese of Rockville Centre: Parish Outreach*, p. 17). The partnership between the agency and the parish is formalized by a written agreement which spells out the responsibilities of the agency and the parish.

The agency agrees to:

- train a parish coordinator

- review and consult through an assigned liaison worker

- help select and train a core group of parishioners

- provide ongoing support

- convene parishes on a regional and diocesan basis

- provide ongoing assessment and review.

The parish agrees to:
- hire a full-time parish coordinator

- provide support and direction for the coordinator

- recruit and develop a core group

- hold weekly meetings with the liaison worker to review cases

- integrate existing parish programs with parish outreach
- participate in convenings
- participate in evaluation and development of parish outreach.

Another characteristic of the agency's structure includes the parish social ministry advisory councils. According to Father Gilmartin, two levels of advisory councils exist, one for the parish and the other diocesan.

The *parish* advisory council, selected by the pastor, coordinator, pastoral staff and parish council, meets at least quarterly to assess needs and ways to meet the needs, review the parish outreach budget, and provide an annual report on the progress of parish outreach.

At the *diocesan* level, the advisory council links the diocese with parish efforts. It advises the diocesan Parish Outreach director regarding local needs and trends; provides ongoing evaluation; recommends future directions, provides input into staffing; acts as a forum for discussion of issues; and convenes diocesan-wide convocations.

"These groups are essential in representing the community, being a resource, and providing needed direction to the parish social ministry team in the parish," Father Gilmartin said. "Representation on this group is significant and influential in implementing necessary projects and focus. To me, this is one of the key groups to be empowered. Parish social ministry belongs to the community and these are the people representing that community. The diocesan advisory council is a resource and support to the director of parish social ministry, which is vital."

The Rockville Centre structure has much to recommend it, particularly its emphasis on quality services through trained social ministers and agency support. Rockville Centre illustrates a commitment to the parish at a very early stage in the development of parish social ministry within the Charities Movement.

Call to Ministry: Alexandria-Shreveport

"Catholic Community Services in Alexandria-Shreveport, La. is a parish social ministry agency," said Sister Brenda Hermann. "Catholic Community Services enables the people to see social ministry as a legitimate church ministry, as the responsibility of all people, especially in the daily circumstances of life. It stresses that all Catholics are missionary, empowers people through training, supervision and recognition of their own giftedness," she explained.

According to Sister Hermann, the concept of Catholic Community Services as an enabler, not a provider, has taken the parishes over three years to accept. Currently, 15 of 86 parishes in the diocese are actively involved in becoming communities of service. "People have been raised in their faith to believe that if they give money to charity, someone else will provide the service. That someone else is usually the Charities social worker," she added.

The primary function of the agency's staff is to assist the parish in discerning its call to social ministry. One of the ways the agency accomplished this was through a series of social ministry workshops held throughout the primarily rural diocese which covers half the state of Louisiana. More than 300 people attended these workshops which emphasized the scriptural roots of social ministry, Church social teachings, Church mission, and the apostolic call of the laity. The agency also stressed moving from the concept of direct aid to social change and the laity's call to social ministry in the world.

"Parishioners identified their own level of awareness of social ministry and then examined the issues within their parish community," Sister Hermann said. Catholic Community Services' staff helped to educate parishioners about social ministry, but they primarily assisted the process of discerning needs and response to need. "Concerns for the unemployed, the aged, the homebound, the need to involve youth in social ministry all surfaced. Even foster homes for pregnant women are seen as a parish response to a social issue," she said.

"To move a diocesan agency to a total parish approach has been a difficult task but one which has begun to take root," Sister Hermann added.

Same Structure, Different Focus: Arlington

Catholic Charities of the Diocese of Arlington illustrates another approach to integrating parish social ministry into the agency. The agency did not change its existing structure so much as change its focus when Father Gerry Creedon became its director in 1982.

"Our agency's change of focus and vision is a basic change, although we didn't decide to abolish any service of the agency," he explained. The change integrated social action, social justice, and parish outreach into the agency's existing operations.

Each existing direct service, including family services, children's service, emergency assistance, etc., was to establish linkage with parishes. In addition, a parish social ministry director joined the agency to assist these efforts and to also develop a social justice thrust to agency activity. After three years, according to Father Creedon, "We're still in the developing stage."

Although the majority of the agency's service programs have initiated some contact with parishes, parish involvement is not total. Father Creedon took a deliberately slow course in introducing a shift in the agency's focus, based on a belief that "developmental change is more effective than a radical shift."

The agency's goals included to:

- provide direct services;

- assess and identify community needs and resources;

- reach out, educate and deepen the involvement of the Christian community;

- facilitate social action and

- work with other community organizations who share common goals.

The agency board of directors, along with the staff and coordinators, got involved in a planning process. "Out of that came **a commitment to develop the parish focus for all the agency services, and to strengthen the consultation and education dimension, linking up and networking with parishes and other community organizations**." Activities now develop in services that implement that direction. For example, children's services developed a family sex education program that hopes to prevent teen pregnancies. Although the activity came out of the experience of children's services, and the initiative came from agency workers, the program developed with parish teens and parish education offices. "The parishioners had decisive input into the development of the program through advisory committees," Father Creedon explained.

Parishes, too, are coming to Catholic Charities to help them develop services. Parishes have hired staff in conjunction with Catholic Charities as well as independently. Parishes are developing parish-based shelter programs. "Whether we were the catalyst or not, we're supportive," added Father Creedon.

In addition to the parish focus of existing agency services, the agency also has a separate parish social ministry office.

"There are three things I've been trying to move toward," explains Beth Long, parish social ministry coordinator.

"First, relationship-building and building constituencies for justice in order to achieve long-term effective action in social ministry. I've watched a lot of little groups not getting anywhere or having any leverage in the county, community or on a diocesan level. I want to concentrate on parish development, uncover new leadership."

Her second goal is to utilize CHD more effectively. "I'm trying to increase the number of local funded groups. We're looking for groups to receive CHD money and to find other sources of money.

"Third is educating and acting toward justice. My bias is on acting, because that's how people learn. One goal is the economic pastoral, and doing peace and justice within a parish context," she said.

"My goal is effective, powerful social ministry through building relationships, developing collective leadership, and educating and acting for justice," she explained.

Because of the agency structure, which has both a parish social ministry office as well as nine other departments that have a parish thrust, there are considerable demands placed on the one-person, parish social ministry office. The parish social ministry office has a broad agenda, including the development of social ministry within the parishes; developing community liaisons; and advancing diocesan peace and justice efforts.

Arlington Catholic Charities has developed a rather unique approach to integrating parish social ministry. For one, the agency has involved parishioners in its policy and program decisions. The agency also focuses its existing services on parish involvement while simultaneously developing social ministry at the parish level. Both efforts, however, utilize the coordination of a parish social ministry office. Because of the dual approach, some problems arise, primarily that it can stretch the agency's parish social ministry office efforts too thin.

In this regard, the agency typifies a common problem faced by other agencies that make parish social ministry an agency focus. That is, how to provide sufficient staff and resources to fully implement its new direction while at the same time continuing agency services. In addition, the agency must achieve a balance in terms of status and priorities between its parish social ministry efforts and existing services. During the transitional phase, some unexpected tensions may arise.

Arlington Catholic Charities continues to meet this challenge.

CONCLUSION

This chapter emphasizes parish social ministry as an essential element of Catholic Charities own mission. A corollary to Charities' mission, of course, is the mission of the local Church and the parishes. The point of convergence for all remains the social mission of the Church. That starting point requires careful consideration while establishing relationships based on mutual respect. "The agency and parish have to share the same philosophy and theology," says Sister Maria Mercedes Hartmann, director of Parish Services with the Aging, Associated Catholic Charities, Baltimore. "We cannot presume that all are on the same wavelength."

Time to connect with each other and to explore a common mission may make the best initial investment for the agency as it reaches out to the parish to develop a partnership in social ministry.

Appendix A

Questions for Analysis

The NCCC Parish Social Ministry Task Force developed the following questions to help agencies, boards, staff and others analyze the degree to which parish social ministry is given the means it needs to succeed. These questions help examine how well parish social ministry (referred to below as PSM) is integrated into the agency. The questions may be asked not only of agency board and staff, but, with modificaton, at the parish level as well.

- What is the role of Catholic Charities (or the parish) in the Church's social mission?
- What is Catholic Charities' role in parish social ministry?
- How does the agency define the parish? Does the agency respect the integrity of the parish, and does it accept the fact that the parish is its own entity?
- What elements of the agency reflect integration of parish social ministry?
- What involvement and relationship does the local community (parish) have regarding the agency decision-making process (e.g. board)?
- How does parish social ministry fit into the mission of the agency? Is it a direction of the agency or a program?
- Is parish social ministry seen as a long-range developmental process that is reflected in the mission, goals, planning, and staff job descriptions?
- Does the agency structure need to be reexamined?
- Does the agency budget reflect the mission? What is PSM share of resources? Are the resources sufficient to the mission?
- What resources—money, space, personnel, public endorsement, homilies, etc.—are allocated to PSM?
- How are PSM staff evaluated and compensated in relationship to other agency staff? What is the relationship of parish social ministry staff in terms of acceptance? Are they a subclass?
- Who are the key people to assure commitment to and continuation of PSM development?

- What is the role of the pastor, parish staff, parish council in development of PSM?
- What is the role of the director in integration efforts?
- Is a planning process used to effect implementation?
- What elements of the agency reflect integration of parish social ministry?
- What are the roadblocks within the agency to integrating PSM?
- Is the energy that propels parish social ministry as strong in the agency as in the parish?
- How does staff development address parish issues?
- How does the parish go beyond its parochial concerns?
- Is collegiality valuable and operable?
- What is occurring in the social environment that may change Catholic Charities and how PSM develops (for example, private philanthropy, industries need for services, megatrends, aging population, etc.)? What are the preferred and probable future?

Appendix B

Addressing Tensions

In reflecting on the relationship between the agency and the parish, recognition should be given to several *tension areas* that may exist within the parish, agency, and community environment. These tensions may include those between men/women; laity/clergy; Charities/other diocesan agencies; parochial/universal church perspectives; Catholic/non-Catholic identity; politics/religion; the powerful/powerless; rich/poor; the churched/unchurched, etc. How do the agency and parish deal with these tensions where they exist?

These considerations need to be addressed at both the parish level as well as at the agency level. In fact, the questions can be used as an educational experience for both parish and agency in gaining greater understanding of their roles in the social mission of the Church, and of the type of relationship they will aim to develop with each other.

Appendix C

Organization Charts

Honolulu
Proposed Diocesan Organization of Social Ministries

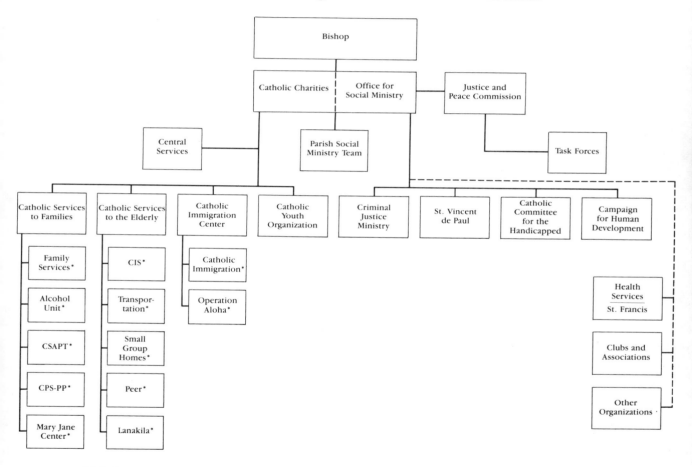

*Existing Unit to be transferred to one of the newly established agencies

Note: Chart depicts administrative relationships and accountability at the diocesan level. It does not show relationships to the vicariates and parishes.

New Hampshire Catholic Charities, Inc.
Organization Chart

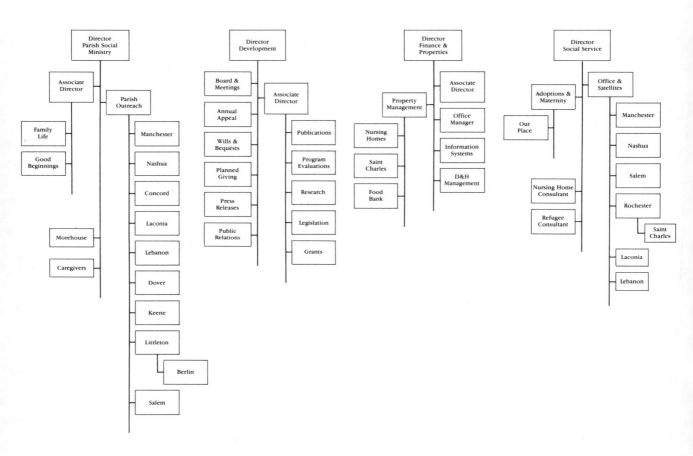

New Hampshire Catholic Charities, Inc.

Parish Outreach Flow Diagram

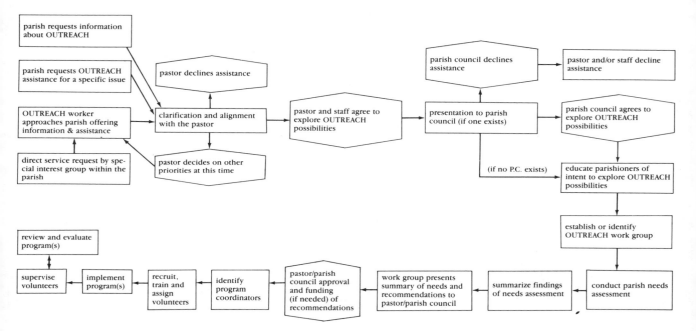

N.B.: This flow diagram is intended to depict the process by which a parish community may explore, develop and implement parish outreach activities. It is a community-building process in which the role of the Parish Outreach worker is to offer guidance and assistance that fosters the community's own ability to recognize and respond to various needs.

Developed by: *Parish Outreach Staff*
New Hampshire Catholic Charities

Catholic Charities of the Diocese of Pittsburgh, Inc.

Organization Chart

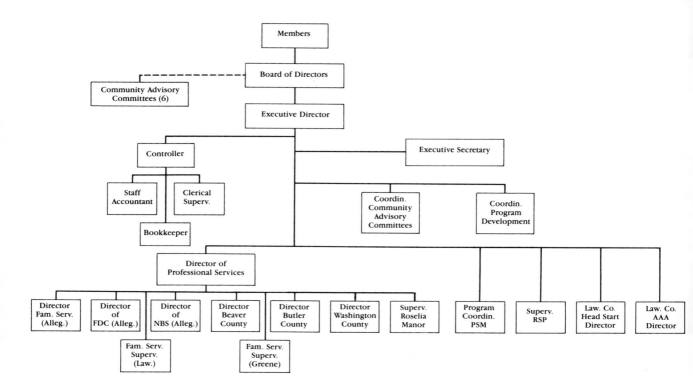

LEGEND

FDC — Family Day Care
NBS — Neighborhood Based Services
CAC — Community Advisory Committees
RSP — Refugee Services Program
PSM — Parish Social Ministry
W/G — Washington/Greene
AAA — Area Agency on Aging

Department of Social Ministry
Alexandria-Shreveport, LA

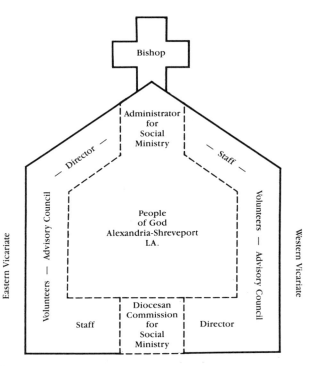

Role Description

Commission for Social Ministry:	Diocesan people who advise, recommend and monitor social ministry development, especially at the parish level.
Advisory Councils:	Vicariate groups, such as CHD, who advise regarding specific concerns or issues.
Volunteers:	People responding to social needs through a. Direct service ministry b. Community development ministry c. Social action ministry d. Parish social ministry coordination
Staff:	People responsible for enabling, training, consultation of parish/community volunteers in social ministry.
Director:	Person responsible for staff and the program design and development on the vicariate level.
Administrator:	Person who liaisons with the bishop and commission regarding the issues, services, programs of the Department—responsible for keeping abreast of trends in social justice, social ministry.

72

Part II:

Doing It

Implementing
Parish Social Ministry

FOUR

The Catholic Charities Agency

Sometimes agencies add parish social ministry, as a self-contained unit, to existing programs without sufficient planning. Questions and conflicts among staff, or other diocesan departments and pastors may then result. What must the agency consider before it implements parish social ministry? What steps can ease the transition toward parish social ministry?

Some factors to review prior to implementing parish social ministry include:

- **the agency mission;**

- **relationship of the agency to the bishop;**

- **diocesan dynamics and intra-diocesan relationships;**

- **parish awareness and perceptions about Catholic Charities;**

- **parish participation in existing agency policy/programs;**

- **agency structure;**

- **expectations and status of parish social ministry;**

- **degree of support for parish social ministry from the agency executive, board, and existing agency staff;**

- **resources allocated to parish social ministry;**

- **and agency parish social ministry staff qualifications, job descriptions, training, and evaluation.**

AGENCY MISSION

An orientation toward the parish must be part of the agency's mission statement. For this reason, it is extremely important to study the agency mission statement and, if necessary, the board, director, and staff should revise it to include parish social ministry.

As previously noted, the recent NCCC *Code of Ethics* declares that the mission of Catholic Charities is to foster the social mission of the Church. The *Code* further defines the ways in which Catholic Charities is to go about its mission: by seeking "full support and participation of the Church as the people of God. . .with diocesan-wide development of parish-based programs of social ministry. . . ."

The parish, then, becomes a way through which the agency fulfills its mission. All agency programs are now viewed in light of the agency mission and in relationship to parish social ministry.

"It must be kept in mind that mission is a statement of values. We must be careful not to include parish social ministry in such a way that it is a title of a program or any other program. The values and principles that underlie parish social ministry as a direction need to be embodied in the mission, not simply a phrase," insists Thomas DeStefano.

Catholic Charities' Relationship with the Bishop Re:the Parish

Probably no other topic regarding parish social ministry receives less attention than that of the relationship between Charities, the bishop, and the parish. In some dioceses, the topic has been purposely avoided. In a few, unarticulated assumptions about the support of the bishop abound, while in others the bishop gives active support to Charities' development of parish social ministry.

Ideally, Charities should have the full enthusiastic support of the bishop in its development of parish social ministry. As a practical matter, Charities needs to know the position of the bishop. Practical because support from the bishop and the understanding of other diocesan agencies and organizations may make diocesan resources more available to parish social ministry. In a few instances, the agency may proceed best by proceeding with its mission implicitly.

76

In a number of dioceses, the bishop has been supportive, sometimes enthusiastically, of Charities' development of parish social ministry.*

There remains, however, a continual need to develop strategies in order to market the concept of parish social ministry to the bishop and other diocesan power sources before, during, and after the agency implements parish social ministry. Diocesan structures remain a fact of life.

Some strategies to use include diocesan workshops at which the bishop or other notables are invited to make a major presentation; inclusion of parish social ministry in the diocesan mission statement; discussion of parish social ministry at priests' senates or deanery/vicariate meetings; articles in the diocesan newspaper or other local media about parish social ministry activities and effectiveness; peer contacts with bishops who support parish social ministry in their dioceses; letter campaigns to the bishop from several parishes about various aspects of parish social ministry; memo flagging of parish social ministry activities from the agency director to the bishop; frank discussion with the bishop and agency director and staff about the benefits of parish social ministry.

The list of possible actions is limited only by the imagination of the agency director and staff. A multi-directed, assertive, and long-term approach is more effective than a one-time single strategy. In any case, shyness affords little access. Who or what has better claim to the bishop's time, energies, and resources?

Intra-diocesan Relationships

More frequently Catholic Charities and other national diocesan agencies and organizations are meeting each other on the parish turf. Sometimes the parish is simply bombarded with diocesan programs. Parish social ministry then may be viewed as just another program. **The need**

(One outstanding example is Bishop Joseph M. Sullivan, Auxiliary Bishop of Brooklyn N.Y, and the episcopal liaison for the National Conference of Catholic Charities, who has frequently spoken and written on parish social ministry. Other dioceses in which the bishop has expressed support of parish social ministry include Rockford; Rockville Centre; Detroit; Oakland; Pittsburgh; Honolulu; Arlington; Covington; Green Bay; Boston; Erie; Albany; Alexandria-Shreveport; Chicago; Galveston-Houston.)

now is one of understanding and interpretation of Charities' **mission at all levels of diocesan structure and creation of a mechanism which allows for effective cooperation among these diocesan groups**. In fact, discussion of cooperative action has begun both locally and at the national level.

Although Catholic Charities' mission encompasses the broad social mission of the Church, in many diocesan structures, other agencies share in part of this mission. Some agencies and groups have narrowly relegated Charities to social services and believe this to be its only realm of activity. But in fact, Charities' activities include both social justice and social service activities.

When ambiguity exits about its role and mission, **Charities should take the initiative in contacting other groups to reach mutual understanding of everyone's mission and establish cooperative actions**. Meeting on a regular basis and establishing a cooperative working relationship with other diocesan groups will stretch resources and produce more effective results. The long-range goal is to assist the develop-

ment of the people of God. Who the actors are in this activity is of less importance.

The development of a diocesan mission statement and plan constitutes one way to clarify relationships and to establish cooperative working relationships. If parish social ministry is not included in the diocesan mission statement/plan, Charities may initiate action for its inclusion. This action would have educational value within the diocesan structure by allowing Charities to define its mission to the local Church and by helping to establish Charities' role more visibly in relationship to the parish.

Relationship with the Parish

Parish Perceptions of Catholic Charities' Role in Parish Social Ministry

In some dioceses, parishioners' knowledge of Catholic Charities may consist only of the annual Charities collection. If that is the case, parishioners may easily develop the idea that by contributing a few dollars each year to Catholic Charities, they fulfill their social responsibility. This points to a limited perception of Charities as doer rather than a catalyst. If such is the case, it suggests that Charities conduct considerable groundwork before engaging in parish social ministry.

It is also interesting to note that in dioceses in which Catholic Charities has successfully implemented parish social ministry, where the parishioners are the doers, that the annual Charities' collection increased dramatically. Brooklyn and Arlington are two prime examples. Brooklyn topped its annual appeal by $200,000 over a three-year period in which the agency shifted its emphasis to parish concerns instead of agency program concerns. In Arlington, after initiating parish social ministry, the annual appeal increased $300,000. In both instances, **the parishes saw Catholic Charities as an agency servicing and empowering the parish rather than a remote agency, much like a foreign missionary, that comes in to take up a collection for the poor "out there."**

Before initiating parish social ministry, it may be well for the agency to take stock of parish perceptions of Catholic Charities and ascertain if parishes see Charities as a service agency to them and as organically linked to the mission of the parish. Subsequent chapters will more fully develop the ways in which Charities inititates contact with the parish.

Mechanisms for Parish Participation in Agency Policy-making

The parish's perception of Catholic Charities relates to mechanisms through which parishioners can participate in the agency's policy-making and programs. Some of these mechanisms include:

- **inclusion of parishioners on the agency board of directors;** *

- **active volunteer recruitment of parishioners and parish organizations for community programs;**

- **welcoming attitude on the part of Charities by identifying with the parish as a partner in the social mission of the Church, and not only acting as a service provider.**

These means allow the parish to experience Catholic Charities and help develop an identity with it. **The relationship between the parish and the agency becomes one of mutual support.** Parishioners may then perceive Charities' work as the work of the parish and vice versa. "By assisting in renewing the parish, however, Catholic Charities also renews itself through the manner in which it serves as the facilitator of a 'new people,'" observes former NCCC Parish Outreach director, Jerome Ernst.

Board and Staff Support for Parish Social Ministry

Role of the Board

The agency's mission statement implies board understanding and acceptance of Charities' role in parish social ministry. If a substantial number of board members have parish identity, their support further en-

---

*The development of a board sometimes receives less than adequate attention, cautions Thomas DeStefano. "Dealing with a board is an art which is not commonly known or practiced well in the not-for-profit field. Catholic Charities is no exception. The development of a board needs more attention if true participation is a real value."

hances Charities' parish social ministry function. Where understanding of Charities' mission is lacking, educating board members about parish social ministry and the mission of Charities is paramount. Board members need to set aside time, *on a regular basis*, to reflect on the mission and goals of the agency. An excellent tool to use for such reflection is the NCCC *Code of Ethics*. Another valuable practice consists of a formalized orientation program about Catholic Charities and its parish mission. Solid board support of and commitment to Charities' mission and parish social ministry will increase the agency's effectiveness.

Role of the Agency Director

The responsibility for implementing parish social ministry lies mainly with the agency director. The support of the executive director is critical to the success of parish social ministry which must be viewed as a total agency direction and priority. To maximize effectiveness, parish social ministry should be directly under the agency director because of the need to coordinate it with all other agency functions as they relate to parishes. If the director considers parish social ministry as one program among many instead of a process through which the agency accomplishes its mis-

sion, then parish social ministry will experience stunted growth and wither without impacting the agency.

The agency director and key staff must not only believe in the power and efficacy of parish social ministry and become its most enthusiastic supporters, but they must also see implementing parish social ministry as their role. For the director is looked at as the chief promotor by staff, the board, the bishop, other agencies, and the broader community. This pivotal position makes the director's attitude toward parish social ministry extremely important, one difficult to camouflage.

"Unless those responsible for the ultimate direction of the organization see themselves as leading the agency in the direction of the values expressed in parish social ministry, then no matter what, it will always be a department," says Mr. DeStefano.

Role of Staff

Thirdly, we must not overlook existing staff. In large, highly structured agencies, introducing parish social ministry as the agency focus becomes a monumental task. As in any organization, major changes in direction produce anxiety and some resistance. Again, staff reflection on the agency's mission provides a positive way to introduce the concept of parish social ministry. Several agencies, as for example, Rockville Centre and Arlington, have applied this approach of staff reflection on the agency's mission and goals with effective results. Staff must see their roles related to parish social ministry and as necessary components to its successful implementation.

AGENCY STRUCTURE

Thinking Parish

The nature of parish social ministry means that it cannot merely be tacked onto existing agency structure. It must be part and parcel of the agency's raison d'etre. Parish social ministry, as stated previously, denotes a process and direction of the agency, not a program. It represents a way of conducting agency business, a way which may or may not be compatible with existing agency programs and methods. The process aspect of parish social ministry presents the most difficulty in implementing, as agencies are program oriented and tend to add parish social ministry as another program component to an already existing structure. But in order to implement parish social ministry, the agency must consider its entire structure.

Structuring parish social ministry into agency operations involves a new way of looking at agency programs. Each agency program becomes a support to parish social ministry, which is now a total agency concern. All agency staff must think parish, in addition to meeting those community needs which may not be feasible within a parish context. But parish social ministry should not be construed as a separate entity within the agency that operates independently of other agency functions.

Parish social ministry as a direction of the agency facilitates social ministry at the parish level. To set up a separate parish social ministry department and then allow it to fend for itself guarantees frustrating parish social ministry efforts. Parish social ministry requires full agency attention if the agency is to fulfill its own mission of empowering the people of God. Within the agency structure, parish social ministry efforts must have authority and power through the direct, visible support of the agency board and executive director. Otherwise, parish social ministry staff fight a double battle: one within the agency to gain appropriate authority to commit the agency to the parishes; and two, convincing parishes to join Charities in a partnership to foster the social mission of the Church.

Expectations of Parish Social Ministry and Agency Resources

Sufficient agency support for parish social ministry in terms of **appropriate authority and resources frequently appears as a major concern** of many agency parish social ministry directors. There is no getting around the fact that parish social ministry is a monumental task. It aims to involve the whole Catholic laity within a diocese through the parish and diocesan structure; it involves other community and ecumenical groups; it involves all the services provided by the agency.

To attempt to continue agency functions in the same manner as before the establishment of parish social ministry also seems unrealistic. The agency can't just "do a little parish social ministry" on the side and continue business as usual because parish social ministry affects almost every aspect of agency operations, primarily in the way it operates, in the manner it functions, in its methodology, in its focus and direction. To do a little parish social ministry sets up failure from the very beginning. The result amounts to a few parishes' involvement in social ministry. Does this really join Catholic Charities in a partnership with the parish to foster the social ministry of the Church? Does this encourage the people of God to respond to their baptismal call to ministry? If Catholic Charities doesn't take on that responsibility, who does?

Parish social ministry by its nature demands a major commitment from the agency in terms of resources and authority. The agency must direct its resources toward involving the parish and parishioners in responding to their baptismal call to ministry. **Parish social ministry does not mean that the agency no longer fulfills social needs in the community. It means that it fulfills them in a *different* way, through a *different* route, and in so doing, may meet more needs than it had been capable of meeting before embarking on parish social ministry.** Is that scary? Indeed. Many agency staff have been trained less in facilitating than in delivering a service. Frequently, the agency structures programs around broad community needs rather than focusing on a more localized response to community needs. Parish social ministry challenges existing agency skills and structures. It also suggests risk be-

cause of a fear that the more visible community needs may not be met, that the needs addressed by the parishes may be too parochial or that parishioners may not be professional enough. **Here, precisely, the skills and comprehensive viewpoint of the agency come to the fore, where the parishes really need what the agency has to offer: to keep the parish in touch with the larger diocesan and universal Church; to finely balance the parochial with the universal; to learn and grow from the interaction with the parish. That indeed poses a challenge**.

Staffing

Eventually, the actual practice of parish social ministry boils down to parish social ministry staff. Staffing patterns differ according to agency size, resources and the personal involvement of the director. Some agencies establish a special staff position or positions to provide the necessary coordination within the agency and to offer the technical assistance to help parishes establish their social ministry. According to NCCC surveys, there are approximately 500 parish social ministry staff in Catholic Charities agencies. There also exist a considerable number of parish social ministry staff at the parish level who are affiliated with Catholic Charities' efforts, as well as some without any Charities' involvement. Discussion here focuses on the agency counterparts (although applicable to the parish staff as well).

The topic of parish social ministry personnel received considerable attention from the NCCC Parish Social Ministry Task Force. They emphasized several factors: the necessity of parish social ministry staff at the agency (and parish) level; qualifications; staff responsibilities; training; evaluation; and just compensation.

Staff Responsibilities

The Midwest Regional Convening participants offered the following as responsibilities of the parish social ministry staff:

- to foster progressive development of parish social ministry;
- to implement priorities;
- to train parishioners in technical skills;

- to coordinate and organize parish social ministry at various levels;
- to model good leadership;
- to give recognition to the importance of parish social ministry in the total structure.

Staff Qualifications

What are the qualifications for parish social ministry staff? This question always poses discussion because of the current developmental stage of the whole field of parish social ministry. However, the NCCC Task Force and the regional participants expressed the following as basic qualifications for parish social ministry staff:

- knowledge of Church social teachings;
- knowledge of parish life;
- commitment to parish social ministry values;
- basic social work practice skills such as interpersonal relationship skills, understanding of human dynamics and behavior, listening skills, communications skills, group leadership skills;
- basic management skills;
- ability to seek out root causes of problems;
- community organization skills;
- broad education in the humanities and social sciences;
- knowledge of community resources, social justice and service groups;
- creativity.

Staff Training

Training agency parish social ministry staff is necessary and needs to be ongoing to clarify or ensure staff understanding of the agency's mission and goals, parish social ministry objectives, agency policy and procedures, and to provide opportunity for support, validation of progress, and discussion of problems.

In addition, specific skills training in areas such as understanding human dynamics and needs, helping skills, leadership development, networking, management, needs assessment, etc. will help meet the stated objectives. Obtaining skills training sometimes presents difficulties, but training is possible through consultation with other agencies, NCCC workshops and convenings, and outside training organizations. Consider budgeting time and money for staff training and make training opportunities available to the parish social ministry staff. All NCCC regional parish social ministry convenings expressed a need for more opportunities to dialogue and share with other parish social ministry personnel in order to counter the feelings of isolation and burnout.

Parish Social Ministry Director

Staff responsibilities involve both intra-agency and parish needs. Within the agency, the parish social ministry director will act as liaison with other agency staff in regard to parish needs, and also coordinate agency/parish activities with other diocesan organizations and groups. The parish social ministry director will also supervise the agency parish social ministry staff who will have direct contact with the parishes in establishing parish social ministry, training parish staff and parishioners, networking with other parishes and community groups, and providing ongoing support and consultation. In some very small agencies, the agency director assumes the role of parish social ministry director. In other agencies, all agency staff comprise the parish social ministry staff, which makes coordination within the agency that much easier.

EVALUATION

The agency director needs to evaluate parish social ministry staff at regular intervals to review progress, determine if staff is meeting its goals, to discern troublesome areas, to affirm agency and staff commitment, and to reward outstanding efforts.

CONCLUSION

The task of implementing parish social ministry within the agency, as we have seen, requires considerable planning and determination. The ramifications are numerous and touch upon every facet of the agency and affect almost all agency relationships, from the bishop, board of directors, to community and national organizations. Commitment to parish social ministry demands significant time, staff, money, and other resources, probably more than most agencies have realized. But it is fair to ask: what are the alternatives?

Sitting Woman

FIVE

Starting Social Ministry in the Parish

Social ministry at the parish level: how is it done?

In the beginning stages, parish social ministry may seem complex and intimidate the novice. But a number of Catholic Charities agencies have developed workable methodologies to implement social ministry at the parish level and their experiences can guide those who are foundering.

This chapter will focus on how the agency introduces and helps develop social ministry in the parish. The discussion here includes a review of the agency's preparations along with the major steps the agency may take to implement social ministry in the parishes. First, we'll look at the agency's initial preparations.

PRELIMINARIES

1. Review Agency Commitment

Before contacting parishes, the agency should review its commitment to parish social ministry. Determine board and staff support, diocesan blessing, and agency allotment of sufficient resources (cf. Chapter Four).

Most importantly, the agency needs to visibly establish its commitment through staff, funding, and administrative support so that parish social ministry energies are fully directed toward the parish and not toward in-house jockeying for acceptance. Full agency support of parish social ministry staff cannot be overemphasized.

2. Research

The agency's parish social ministry director and staff need basic knowledge about the parishes in the diocese or area. Familiarity with the parishes and knowledge about their locations, size, neighborhood (urban, suburban, rural), demographics, or any striking social conditions such as high unemployment, crime, drugs, alcoholism, etc. proves helpful for planning.

Develop parish profiles. Establish a file for every parish/pastor, if possible, or if not, for those likely to undertake social ministry. Add information as you progress. Collect pertinent information such as parish size, name of pastor, etc. from the appropriate diocesan office, diocesan parish directory and, for demographics, from census statistics.

Other sources of parish data include the diocesan newspaper files, newspaper clippings, parish fliers, anniversary sketches, histories, etc. Interview diocesan departments or agencies for their knowledge of parishes based on their experiences. (For example note which parish may have outstanding liturgies, an active school association, etc.). All research need not be done before implementing parish social ministry, but establish a systematic way of collecting data. This knowledge becomes useful when the agency staff begins to contact the parishes.

Know the pastors. Include whatever information is available on the pastor in the parish file. He will undoubtedly react more favorably during your first interview if you acknowledge his work in ecumenism or comment on the fine job he's done as a past committee chairman. **Knowledge is power**.

3. Plan

Develop a preliminary plan, even if it must be revised after your first parish experience. The plan acts as a guide, a roadmap to where you want

to go. Develop an agency plan for the diocese, regions, counties, neighborhoods, and, as you progress, for individual parishes. Set up goals and objectives which will help evaluate agency progress in the realization of parish social ministry in the diocese. Include strategies and tentative schedules in your planning. Impose specificity if revision is needed. Planning helps you think through what to do and how to do it. It helps you keep on course, and be more efficient and effective.

4. *Review Elements for Implementing Social Ministry in the Parish*

These elements serve as guidelines to the agency in implementing social ministry within the parishes:

- **approach**—general or targeted?

- **pastor contact**

- **parish leadership contacts**

- **preparing and educating the parish about social ministry**

- **needs assessment options**

- **resource assessments**

- **contracting with the parish**

- availability and training of **social ministry staff** at the parish level

- recruitment and training of parish social ministry **volunteers**

- **process models** (teams, committees, action for justice, service, values, etc.)

- **parish goal setting**

- **parish plan for action**

- **collaborating and networking** with other parishes/groups

- **implementing** parish plan

- **assessing and evaluating**

The above guidelines focus on the agency acting directly or assisting the parish in its action.

These four steps—*agency commitment, research, planning, and review of implementation guidelines*—will help smooth the process for the PSM staff as they begin the monumental task of implementing social ministry in the parishes. Let us examine the implementation guidelines more closely.

GUIDELINES TO IMPLEMENTING SOCIAL MINISTRY IN PARISHES

1. *Approach to the Parishes: General or Targeted?*

Should you take a shotgun or targeted approach? Do you convene a diocesan workshop on parish social ministry and send out flyers to all the parishes to announce your availability for consultation? Or do you zero in on one or two parishes without fanfare and establish a track record?

Your approach depends on a great many factors: staff and available resources; ability to network several parishes or groups of parishes at one time; past experience in parish social ministry; knowledge and confidence; and parish readiness for social ministry.

General Approach

For the more experienced, a shotgun approach in which you hang up your sign, tickle potential parishes with workshops and invitations and proceed simultaneously with several parishes, may work just fine.

In this approach, the agency may convene a diocesan-wide workshop to which all parishes are invited to participate. **Diocesan-wide conferences are an excellent mechanism to introduce parish social ministry if the agency is thoroughly prepared to immediately implement its plans.** The conference motivates or interests parishes to seriously begin social ministry. The conference should also make Charities highly visible and impress that Catholic Charities is available to help.

In the planning and presentation of the conference, involve agency staff, other diocesan divisions, and parishes as resources. A typical agenda may include an address by the bishop; a session on the theology and concept of parish social ministry; speakers from other agencies and dioceses experienced in parish social ministry; speakers identified from the national Catholic Charities office and its Parish Social Ministry Advisory Committee; and small, how-to group workshops on topics such as conducting a needs assessment, recruiting parish volunteers, developing parish leadership, etc.

Prior to the conference, before convening the parishes, the agency should have its follow-up plans and next steps firmly in place. Unfortunately, agencies sometimes do not prepare the next steps. In the past, a wave of parish social ministry diocesan workshops were conducted without adequate follow-through, or sufficient agency commitment of staff and resources, resulting in raised, but later frustrated, hopes and expectations.

Targeted Approach

For the novice, a targeted approach to parish social ministry is probably more realistic than an initial diocesan-wide approach. The diocesan convening may have greater impact after the agency gains some experience and is prepared with follow-up plans. If you are building a reputation, testing your own know-how, establishing your authority in parish social ministry, and creating a history, the first parish experience is particularly critical. Success attracts.

2. *Preparation and Strategy for Contacting the Pastor*

Whether working quietly with one parish or developing several parishes simultaneously, the initial contact with the parish usually takes place through the pastor. The pastor and assistant pastors are key to the development of parish social ministry and if it is to happen at all, they must agree to it. At the very least, they shouldn't oppose it. The pastor's blessing and whole-hearted support are preferable as it will allow him the opportunity to exhibit the leadership that the local church community expects.

Agency practitioners experienced in establishing clergy contacts offer the following advice for gaining pastor support:

- **research parishes** and pastors to determine which seem open;
- **become visible** to pastors;
- **use peers to influence the pastor**, especially other pastors connected with successful social ministry efforts;
- **identify parishioners** who are sympathetic to parish social ministry and who may influence the pastor; (depending on the circum-

94

stances, you may want to see the pastor with parish leadership to avoid a negative response at first contact);

- **listen to the pastor's needs** and present your proposal to meet his concerns;

- **approach the pastor with respect** and a positive attitude;

- emphasize that **pastor involvement** in the process is flexible, depending on his time and interest;

- **be non-threatening**;

- **explain the partnership advantage with Catholic Charities**, for example, availability of professional training, and the assurance of quality service through the application of Charities' knowledge and methodology;

- **appeal to the Gospel call to justice**;

- emphasize practical **advantages of parish social ministry** to parish leadership and to the pastor, for example:
    renewal of the faith community
    increased lay involvement
    possibilities for ecumenical cooperation
    re-energized parish community
    outreach to those in need
    utilization of untapped resources
    increased ability to raise money for local services
    positive public relations with community
    assistance to the parish in fulfilling its mission
    participation in universal Church mission;

- and most importantly, **listen**.

3. *Strategy for Involving Parish Leadership*

In addition to the pastor's and associates' leadership, obtain cooperation of other parish leaders such as staff, parish council, and leaders of parish organizations. These persons may or may not emerge as the social ministry leadership later, but because of their office, they are owed the courtesy of an introduction and invitation to participate in social ministry. They may also refer other potential parishioners for training in parish social ministry processes.

Group and individual meetings with established parish leaders offer Catholic Charities the opportunity to listen to the parish and to get to know the concerns of the parishioners. The group meetings also allow Charities to introduce itself and its purpose; to explain parish social ministry; to involve the leaders in the process; to allay fears; to obtain referrals for potential social ministry leaders; to help build consensus for social ministry within the parish; and to build a relationship between the parish and Catholic Charities. Place special emphasis on the fact that parish social ministry belongs to the parish and that Catholic Charities is there to listen and assist the parish in its efforts.

4. *Preparing and Educating the Parish About Social Ministry*

Introducing social ministry to the parish may proceed in a general way before a more intensive process begins. Early on stress the spiritual and communal aspects of social ministry to the entire parish. Too frequently, parish social ministry gets relegated to a social concerns committee, when in fact, social ministry belongs to all the parishioners. Parishioners should have as much opportunity to participate in social ministry as they do in the liturgical and educational functions of the parish. **Social ministry should be presented to the entire parish in the context of a legitimate parish function to which all members of the community are called to respond**. Parishioners should have an opportunity to gain an understanding of social ministry as a response to their baptismal call and the Gospel teachings.

Social ministry makes a great topic for homilies, special liturgies, small workshops, and adult education discussions. These and other means which help prepare a positive environment set the stage for a more intensive involvement in social ministry.

Stress throughout that social ministry belongs to the parish community and that it is *not* a Catholic Charities' program. Explain that Chari-

ties offers assistance to the parish in developing its mission and ministry in communion with the local Church.

5. Needs Assessment Options

Parish discernment of parish/community needs may involve a number of assessment options, from simple surveys to elaborate group interviewing research. A needs assessment aims to identify pertinent factors regarding a social or community need. These factors include the specific need, those who have the need, reasons for the need, the severity of the need, ways the need may be filled (including personnel, resources, facilities, costs, time requirements), potential resistance to filling the need, and means to overcome resistance. (See samples of needs assessments in Appendix).

6. Resource Assessment

Resource assessment here refers to potential resources available to the parish, which may include the parishioners themselves, neighborhood and local organizations, funding sources, and private and government programs. Determine resources for the total social ministry effort as well as for particular needs. Assessing available resources permits a realistical appraisal of social ministry actions and direction.

Not to be overlooked is the Catholic Charities agency which has professional resources for problems that the parishes may be reluctant to identify. For example, situations involving interpersonal issues such as alcoholism, marital problems, family violence may exist in the community. Or there may be situations that require intervention from the legal and public welfare systems for serious emotional problems such as neglect of children or abuse. Catholic Charities has an awareness of these service systems of which parishioners sometimes need to be aware. The parish can become involved in these services by supporting these professional services in many ways such as referral or by offering short-term shelter.

7. *Contracting with the Parish*

Once the agency has gained a sense of parish readiness to develop social ministry, it is usually advisable to prepare a contract between the agency and parish. A number of agencies provide contracts in which the responsibilites of the parish and the agency are spelled out. The Chicago Archdiocese Parish-Community Services Department of Catholic Charities, under the direction of Sister Shirley Fineran, O.S.F., has developed contract-making to a high degree. Rockville Centre Charities develops a partnership agreement with the parishes. (Examples of their contracts and agreements are included in the Appendix at the end of this chapter).

Customize contracts for each parish, particularly in terms of the services and responsibilites of each party. Include standard features such as the names of the contracting parties; responsibilites of each party (spell out exactly what the agency will do and what the parish will do; for example, the agency will develop a needs assessment plan and train parishioners, while the parish will hire a social ministry coordinator); amount and manner of payment for services; method for canceling; signatures of person authorized to sign contracts for each organization; date; and the time span during which the contract is in force. Seek legal consultation in the initial development of contracts.

8. *Availability and Training of Social Ministry Staff at the Parish Level*

Many parishes have full or part-time staff for music and religious education. Likewise, parishes need staff for social ministry. In the past, volunteer coordinators took responsibility for this function. But ideally, a trained, accountable social ministry staff person can more adequately perform the coordinating, motivating, administrative and training aspects of social ministry. Small parishes or rural parishes that lack sufficient resources may prefer to share a parish social ministry coordinator. They may also seek outside funding from foundations, local CHD, or hold special fundraising activities to help finance social ministry.

Past experience has shown that the agency should not provide staff to the parish for several reasons. First, the expense of furnishing social ministry staff to every parish in a diocese is prohibitive. In some large agencies, Catholic Charities provides *regional* parish social ministry coordinators who support and train the parish's social ministry staff. Secondly, since social ministry belongs to the parish, the parish's social ministry staff should be accountable to the parish rather than to the agency. The agency should very actively encourage each parish to staff a qualified social minister or to share a social minister with one or more parishes. If paid social ministry staff simply is not feasible, the parish may contract with Charities to train and develop volunteer coordinators.

Training social ministry staff *in the parish* needs emphasizing. Here, Charities plays a major role, for it has the skills, knowledge, experience and resources to provide training in the key parish social ministry processes. As the preeminent human service division of the Church, Catholic Charities offers a valuable service to the parishes through its training capacities. In recent years, Charities has placed renewed emphasis on

this catalyst-like function. Catholic Charities' theological, spiritual, and practical dimensions prove invaluable in training parish staff and assisting parishes to develop their local social ministry.

9. *Review Process Models*

Parish social ministry takes many forms as each parish community expresses its unique gifts and needs. However, some basic forms of social ministry have common characteristics. These processes concern primarily direct services, primarily social action, or combined service/action. Convening the community marks the first step toward service or action.

Ultimately, each process aims to serve people in need while developing community. The difference between the direct service and social action models lies in the *source and manner of* fulfilling needs. **In either case, however, the participants should experience a bonding, unity, and sense of community**.

Direct Service. Direct service frequently emerges as the first expression of social ministry. Here, parishioners take responsibility to deliver service to those in need. Parish services vary, from bereavement counseling to providing transportation to the elderly for shopping.

Parish social ministry emphasizes that parishioners determine the service, arrived at through a process of **parishioner discernment**. The **parishioners become the doers**. Ministry implies more than social services. Parish social **ministry** does *not* mean that the parish hires a sister who decides that the elderly need telephone assurance and then proceeds to telephone them regularly. Legitimate parish social ministry requires that parishioners become involved in assessing and filling the need.

Social Action. When social action results from parishioner discernment, it may mean that the need cannot be filled by the parish alone. Social action, as well as direct service, applies the principle of subsidiarity, which aims to fill a need at the most localized level of social responsibility. Parishioners may discover that a need demands greater resources than the parish can provide and so they seek greater community support. For example, parishioners do not have the authority to install a traffic light at a busy intersection, but their joint action may convince proper authorities to provide that needed service. Or at another level, parishioners may organize with others to lobby state representatives to pass legislation that provides fuel assistance to low income families. And still at another level, organized parishioners may join with other groups to save Social Security benefits. In any case, **the communal process of social action emphasizes group discernment and group action** as the primary elements of this form of social ministry.

Combined direct service/social action. In most instances, social ministry within the parish will develop along the lines of both service and action. Sometimes there arises a question of antagonism between the two kinds of activities. Parish social ministry does not admit to an inherent difference in value between the two types of activity. Rather, each complements the other and both are necessary. Social action, because it does not afford immediate satisfaction and requires a long-range view, may need special efforts to sustain parishioners during times of slow progress.

These processes receive greater attention in subsequent chapters.

10. Parish Goal Setting and Planning

Part of the parish social ministry process involves parishioners setting clear, specific and realistic goals; setting priorities; discussing strategies; and planning how to achieve the goals. The parish's social ministry staff coordinates these efforts, encourages and trains parishioners, and keeps the process on course.

11. *Implementing the Parish Plan*

Action follows the assessment of needs and resources, goal setting and planning. The parish should respond according to its capabilities to accomplish the action, either by itself or in conjunction with other churches and community organizations.

12. *Collaborating and Networking with Other Parishes/Groups*

Networking among parishes has developed as one of the more important concepts in parish social ministry. In networking, parishes pool resources and effectively increase their power by uniting with others. Catholic Charities plays a pivotal role in networking, for it can easily link parishes that work along similar lines. Advantages of networking or clustering, include increased resources, mutual sharing, support, infusion of new ideas, expansion and growth of goals and means, increased learning and training opportunities, and rejuvenation. Networking and clustering in social ministry are highly recommended and, in most instances, preferable to singular parish social ministry efforts because of the increased opportunity to overcome parochial limitations through outside contacts.

13. Assessing and Evaluating

Periodically, throughout the social ministry activities, both the agency and the parish coordinators should take time to assess progress, to check if the goals are in sight, or perhaps have shifted, to affirm progress, to evaluate strategies, re-group, strengthen weak areas, and give support. At the parish level, seek parishioners' input in evaluations. How often assessments occur depends on the agency's staffing resources, the number of parishes involved and other factors. Philadelphia parish social ministry workers meet with Charities' supervisors every three weeks to evaluate progress and discuss concerns. Evaluations at the agency and parish levels by the directors or coordinators offer opportunitities to nourish the social ministers or parishioners in the social ministry process, to take stock, and begin anew.

SUMMARY

In summary, the key steps the agency takes to implementing social ministry at the parish level include:

- review of **agency commitment**;
- determining the **approach**;
- **contacting the pastor** and parish leadership;
- preparing and **educating the parish** about social ministry.

The agency also works with or assists the parish in the following steps:

- performing **needs and resource assessments**;
- **contracting** with the parish;
- obtaining and **training** social ministry **staff** at the parish level;
- **recruiting and training** parish social ministry **volunteers**;
- reviewing service and social action for justice **process models**;
- setting **goals and planning**;
- collaborating and **networking** with other parishes/groups;
- **implementing** the parish plan;
- and **evaluating**.

Appendix A

Samples of Needs Assessments

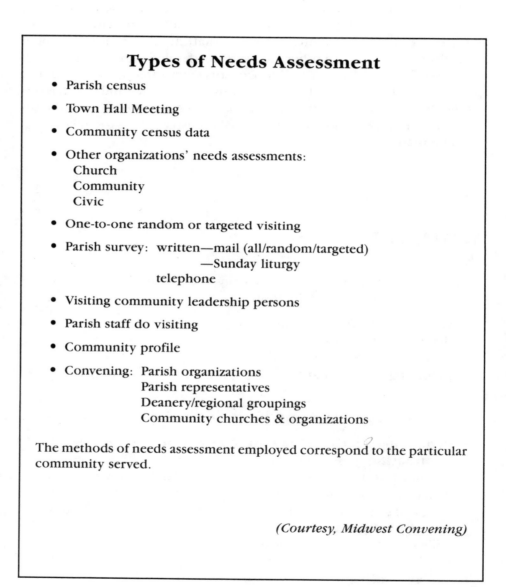

Types of Needs Assessment

- Parish census

- Town Hall Meeting

- Community census data

- Other organizations' needs assessments:
  Church
  Community
  Civic

- One-to-one random or targeted visiting

- Parish survey: written—mail (all/random/targeted)
  —Sunday liturgy
  telephone

- Visiting community leadership persons

- Parish staff do visiting

- Community profile

- Convening: Parish organizations
  Parish representatives
  Deanery/regional groupings
  Community churches & organizations

The methods of needs assessment employed correspond to the particular community served.

(Courtesy, Midwest Convening)

Survey Methods

Method	Description	Requirements	Benefits	Disadvantages
Telephone Survey	Callers ask questions and record data	• Telephone listing of audience • Trained surveyors • Telephone equipment	• Accuracy of data recording by trained staff • If well organized, can be quick and personal approach	• Time consuming or even inappropriate for use with long questionnaire and/or extremely large audience
Mail Survey	Survey questionnaire is mailed to audience and returned by mail	• Accurate mailing list for audience • Precise and clear written instructions for respondents	• Can yield adequate and quick response	• Mailing preparation and costs • Approach is less personal • Never yields 100% return
Door-to-Door Survey	Survey staff deliver questionnaire, record responses at audience homes	• Accurate address list or definition of "territory" • Trained interview staff	• Very personal approach • Accuracy of data recording by trained staff	• Time consuming • Costly if paid interviewers used
Survey at Mass	Survey distributed, completed and returned at Mass	• Brief and simple survey form	• Immediate return of data	• Cannot reach non-practicing Catholics, shut-ins, etc.

(Courtesy, Archdiocese of Baltimore
Division of Research and Planning)

Needs Assessment and Consequent Planning Process

Ideally, **Needs Assessment** is followed by short and long-range planning based on the establishment of priorities. It is a **process** of 1) Study and 2) Action. All members do not participate in all of the process, but the Parish and Parish Council/Ministry Committee covers all, brings it all together.

I. **Study**: Assessment of **Needs** and **Resources**: This will give a profile of parish

    A. **Needs**
- 1. Interview, using same format, parish leaders, staff, pastor
- 2. Questionnaire to selected persons, randomly, or those at weekend liturgies, etc. Make certain yours reflects ideas, suggestions of the Committee. ALWAYS PRE-TEST QUESTIONNAIRES!
- 3. Take into consideration the larger community of which parish is a part—i.e., what problems found in this area—drug, abused persons, etc.

    B. **Resources**
- 1. Parish service inventory—committees, organizations.
- 2. Develop resource bank of individual parishioner service: plumber, doctor, carpenter, teacher, etc., to meet emergency needs, possibly to develop coordinated program.
- 3. Neighborhood, community resources: senior centers, community organizations, etc.
- 4. Agency resources, local DSS office, state, federal programs, health facilities, etc.
- 5. Surface what is already being done on individual basis, personal commitment, at meetings, liturgies, etc.

    C. **Analysis**: Use three (3) columns, or some other device containing

           NEEDS   RESOURCES   ACTION
- 1. Prior to listing on grid, enter each Need and Resource on separate cards.
- 2. Categorize Needs broadly: i.e.,

                FOOD—meals, emergency supply, etc.
                FUNDS—medicine, gas & electric, rent, etc.
                SAFETY—street lights, crossings, trash pick-up
- 3. Sift through Resource cards, extract all which could be applied to Need category.
- 4. Enter into grid, Need category and opposite it, all appropriate Resources.
- 5. Use the completed sheet to develop Action options (if any!) then prioritize options.
- 6. **Analysis** is completed when decision is made regarding which Needs to work on first.

II. Now You Are Ready for Action! Blessings!

(Courtesy, Parish Services with the Aging
Associated Catholic Charities
Baltimore, MD)

Needs Assessment Tool for Parish Staff, Council, Committees

General Information

1. Number of families in your parish? _____

2. Number of persons in the parish? _____

3. Number of people, non-Catholics included, within parish boundaries? _____

4. Age distribution: within parish   within parish boundaries

   Up to 5, incl.   _____   _____
   6 to 14   _____   _____
   15 to 19   _____   _____
   20 to 44   _____   _____
   45 to 64   _____   _____
   65 to 80   _____   _____
   81 and over   _____   _____

5. Average age of adult parishioners? _____

6. Estimated family income of those living within the boundaries—an estimated average? $ _____

7. Estimated annual income of parish families? $ _____

8. Average education of parish family heads—check one:
   some grade school _____   some high school _____   some college _____
   college degree _____   higher than college _____

9. Racial, ethnic background of families within parish boundaries:
   # Black _____   # White _____   # Asian _____
   # Hispanic _____   # Caribbean _____

10. Religious background of families within parish boundaries:
    # Protestant _____   # Catholic _____   # Jewish _____   # Other _____

11. What is the most common social problem for which the Staff's help is asked?
    _____

12. What is the greatest social concern of the parishioners? _____
    _____

13. Does the whole neighborhood share this concern? _____

14. What community resources are available to address these problems? _____
    _____ Adequate? _____

15. In your opinion, for which problem should the parish work on? _____
    _____

Name _____

Address _____ Phone _____

*(Courtesy, Parish Services with the Aging
Associated Catholic Charities
Baltimore, MD)*

Needs Assessment

Social Action

The purpose of the Social Action Committee shall be to examine and advise on such matters as race relations, housing, crime, drugs, political issues, and other social actions affecting our society; to assist in the education of parishioners in the principles of a genuinely Christian social philosophy.

I. Personal or Family Needs:

Please check **five** areas which you feel that you, or any member of your family may need help with, and that our parish should provide.

1. _____ Child Management
2. _____ Single Parent Experience
3. _____ Loneliness
4. _____ Death and Dying
5. _____ Sex Education
6. _____ Separation/Divorce
7. _____ Communication in the Family
8. _____ Coping with Stress
9. _____ Mid-life Experience
10. _____ Aging Experience
11. _____ Learning to Forgive
12. _____ Caring for an Older Person

II. Neighborhood Situation Needs:

Please check the issues in which you feel your neighborhood has problems and with which our parish should provide help.

1. _____ Drug Abuse
2. _____ Alcoholism
3. _____ Theft
4. _____ Gangs
5. _____ Peer Pressure
6. _____ Materialism
7. _____ Unemployment
8. _____ Isolation
9. _____ Sexual Promiscuity
10. _____ Elitism

B. As a parish community should we address any of these problems?
_____ Yes _____ No Please explain: _____
_____

III. Parish Community Needs:

Please check the areas of need that you feel are **not** being met by the parish.

1. _____ Home visits for elderly and shut-ins
2. _____ Temporary homemaker services
3. _____ Counseling: Marital, Family, Individual
4. _____ Transportation to appointments, shopping, etc.
5. _____ Emergency food
6. _____ Emergency clothing
7. _____ Child care
8. _____ Adult education on social issues
9. _____ Informal job bank: e.g., car repair in exchange for child care, house repair, etc.
10. _____ Money for temporary financial emergencies
11. _____ Support groups: e.g., Single Parents, Abusive Parents, Separated-Widowed-Divorced

*(Courtesy, St. Bernadette Parish
Baltimore, MD
from Parish Survey)*

Parish Needs Assessment

Name _____ Phone _____

Address _____ Age _____

Please answer the following questions and place an "X" to the left of those activities you would like to actively participate in.

Worship
In what ways could our liturgies be enhanced? (planning, music, lay participation, decorations, etc.)

_____

_____

_____

Education
What types of education would you like our parish to offer? (parenting, scripture, peace and justice, tutoring, prayer seminars, etc.)

_____

_____

_____

Service Ministry
How can the needs of the poor, grieving, lonely, and/or elderly best be addressed in our parish? (in addition to our present services)

_____

_____

_____

Building Community
How can we help to build a stronger sense of community among the members of our parish and our neighbors?

_____

_____

_____

(Courtesy, Catholic Charities of the Archdiocese of Chicago)

Detailed Needs Assessment Questionnaire

Below are listed some of the needs that are commonly experienced by people within a community. Look at the list and place a check by those you feel most significantly exist within our community. Add any that are not listed. At the bottom of this sheet please write those three needs that you think are most critical.

_____ Loneliness

_____ Unemployment

_____ Substance abuse (alcohol/drugs)

_____ Transportation

_____ Race relations

_____ Housing (cost/quality/discrimination)

_____ Day care (preschool, middle school, elderly)

_____ Medical care availability

_____ Food/Clothing

_____ Environmental needs

_____ Utilities

_____ Family relations (communication, stages of growth, alienation, etc.)

_____ Recreation

_____ Abuse (spouse, child, parent)

_____ Government (ineffective at local, stage, national level)

_____ Welfare

_____ Education

_____ Legal services availability

_____ Rural life services

_____ _____

_____ _____

_____ _____

Please list your three most prominent needs:

_____

_____

_____

(Courtesy, Catholic Family Service, Lubbock, TX)

Informal Needs Assessment for Elderly

1. Ask group what they perceive the needs of the elderly to be.

2. Ask other groups and individuals what they perceive as the needs:
   • Parish priests and staff
   • Police
   • Welfare office, Social Security representatives
   • Council on Aging
   • Other agency representatives that serve the elderly
   • Senior citizen groups
   • Possible census information
   • Eucharistic Ministers that visit shut-ins

3. Needs of elderly:
   • Transportation to church, store, doctor, etc.
   • Grocery shopping
   • Home repairs, yard clean-up
   • Home care
   • Telephone reassurance
   • Visiting (Adopt a Grandparent, or Friendly Visiting Program)
   • Letter-writing
   • Recreational programs
   • Nutritional programs (Meals on Wheels)
   • Placement in facilities for the aged
   • Medicare and insurance counseling
   • Advocacy for various services
   • Legislation benefiting elderly
   • Preparation for death
   • Housing
   • Social gatherings at church: Mass, card party, dinner, etc.

4. If asking elderly themselves what they perceive as their needs, look for names of individuals in:
   • Census
   • Communion Call List
   • Call Council on Aging
   • Call Easter Seals
   • Ask parishioners at Mass to give name, address, and phone of an elderly person they know that needed a service or a visit.

(Courtesy, Associated Catholic Charities of New Orleans, Inc.)

Appendix B

Sample Contracts and Agreement

Sample Contract

This agreement is entered into this _____ day of

_____ , 19_____ , between Catholic Charities,
Parish-Community Services, 645 West Randolph Ave., Chicago, Illinois, hereinafter called

"Consultant," and/or "Supervisor," and _____

of _____ parish,

(address) _____ , hereinafter

called "Administrator," and including _____ ,

coordinator, hereinafter called "Consultee," and/or "Supervisee."

(Courtesy, Catholic Charities of the Archdiocese of Chicago)

Contract for a Program of Parish-Community Services

This agreement is entered into this _____ day of _____ , 19____ , between Catholic Charities Parish-Community Service Program, 645 W. Randolph Ave.,

Chicago, Illinois hereinafter called the "Supervisor," and _____

_____

of _____ parish,

(address) _____ ,

hereinafter called "Administrator," and including _____

_____ , coordinator, hereafter called the "Supervisee."

This agreement includes all the elements of Phase III, as spelled out in the contract agreement; stipulating the responsibilities of both parties to this agreement.

EVALUATION
At the end of the contract year, both parties will evaluate progress toward completion of goals.

TERMINATION
The agreement may be terminated by either party sixty (60) days or more prior to the termination of agreement, following delivery of written notice of intent to terminate.

PAYMENT OF SERVICES
The cost reimbursed to Catholic Charities for this service will be _____ dollars, equal amounts to be paid monthly/quarterly, as agreed upon. This payment for service to

begin September _____ through August 19____ .

DIRECTOR/SUPERVISOR _____

ADMINISTRATOR _____

SUPERVISEE _____

(Courtesy, Catholic Charities of the Archdiocese of Chicago)

CATHOLIC CHARITIES, ROCKVILLE CENTRE PARTNERSHIP AGREEMENT*

Catholic Charities	Parish
• Introduces Outreach to Parish; explains basic concepts; outlines procedures, including a profile of qualifications of personnel. • Presentation of Partnership Agreement.	• Through pastor and staff, explores the concept, examines Parish resources. • Acceptance of Partnership.

> • Partnership formed.
> • Catholic Charities and the Parish start a search for candidates for the Parish Outreach Coordinator position mutually acceptable to the parish and Catholic Charities.

Catholic Charities	Parish
• Trains the Coordinator in areas deemed necessary, such as personal skills, administration of Outreach, and knowledge of resources. Twelve-Session Orientation and ongoing seminars.	• Pastor hires a full-time Parish Outreach Coordinator.
• Catholic Charities provides a professional review of cases and consultation on program development by assigning a Liaison Worker to the parish.	• Pastor and Parish Staff provide support and direction to Coordinator through Staff meeting.
• Aids in the development of Core group by providing assistance in selection, a screening process, and training.	• Recruitment and development of Core group.
• Community Life Center provides Coordinator with ongoing support and discussion of local issues at monthly meetings. Parish Outreach administration provides diocesan monthly support meetings.	• Coordinator schedules weekly meeting to review cases with Liaison Worker at the parish.
• Defines and reinforces the roles of existing service groups and organizations, e.g., Society of St. Vincent de Paul and Legion of Mary.	• Integrates Outreach with existing programs in Parish which are essential to proper coordination of resources, locally.
• Convening of Parishes on a regional and diocesan basis for support and direction.	• Pastor or his delegate and Parish Outreach Coordinator participate in meetings as convened.
• Ongoing assessment and review as to the needs of Parish and response of Catholic Charities.	• Monthly and Annual evaluation of the development of Outreach in the parish.

> • GOAL—Convening of Catholic Charities and parishes as an expression of the life of the Church on Long Island.

_____   _____
Director—Parish Outreach   Pastor

_____   _____
Regional Administrator   Parish Coordinator

_____
(Date)

*Reprinted with permission from *A Parish Social Ministry in the Diocese of Rockville Centre: Parish Outreach*.

Appendix C

Samples

Guidelines for Volunteers
Guidelines for Friendly Visitors
Core Group Responsibilities
Volunteer Job Descriptions
Volunteer Application

*(Courtesy, Catholic Charities of the
Archdiocese of Chicago)*

St. Timothy Parish
Chicago, IL

St. Timothy Enabling Ministry (STEM)
Guidelines for Volunteers

Persons interested in being volunteers in St. Timothy Enabling Ministry (STEM) will sign up for service on the first and second Sundays in March of each year. Sign-up forms will be included in the church bulletin on these two Sundays. Completed sign-up forms will be deposited in the STEM box at the rear of the church or brought to the rectory.

Volunteers are asked to attend approximately four general meetings to be scheduled throughout the year. The purpose of these meetings will be twofold:

to discuss any questions/concerns which may have arisen and to maintain mutual support

to provide education/information on relevant topics.

Commitment on the part of each volunteer is open-ended. A volunteer's name, therefore, will remain on the active list from year-to-year unless s/he specifically requests removal.

Job descriptions for each of the STEM service areas will be provided.

Persons requesting service will contact the STEM coordinator at the rectory. (See church bulletin for specifics.)

116

Our Lady of Mt. Carmel Church
Melrose Park, Illinois 60160

CASA Guidelines for Friendly Visiting

1) Who Will We Serve?

a) Food Pantry follow-ups
b) Referrals from area hospitals
c) Referrals from parish (i.e. Communion Lists)
d) Referrals from Proviso Council On Aging

Our basic aim is to serve those seniors and homebound shut-ins living in the Melrose Park area and/or parish area.

2) How Often Do We Visit?

Usually once a week for the average of about one hour.

3) What Kinds of Things Will a Visitor Do?

The goal of the visitor is to provide companionship by talking and listening to the client. There should be no chores, no giving out medication, no shopping, and no involvement with financial things.

4) Why and What Do We Hope to Accomplish?

We want to establish a relationship with the person we visit that says we care for you and are interested in you.

5) What Kind of Reporting Must Be Done?

Every month you will be asked to mail in a written log (report) of your visits to the coordinator of the program. (Please see the log report sheet.) You will also be asked to attend periodic volunteer meetings once every two months.

Responsibility Sheet for CASA Core Group

1) **Liaison for CASA in Action Program:**
    a) To attend all core group and volunteer meetings.
    b) To provide spiritual support for the CASA ministry, the core group and the volunteers.
    c) To provide assistance to volunteers to meet special needs or problems which arise for those being served. (Problem-solving and decision-making.)
    d) To offer administrative suggestions to Coordinator and Core Group.
    e) To edit publicity and special correspondence connected with the CASA program.
    f) To serve as coordinator for special events with a designated chairperson.
    g) To serve as "intake person" for initial calls requesting services.

2) **Coordinators/Chairpersons of Meetings:**
    a) To coordinate all volunteer meetings.
    b) To conduct all meetings of volunteers.
    c) To coordinate a method of archiving the CASA program (book containing minutes, bulletins, special events, correspondence, publicity, statistics, etc.)
    d) Coordinate scheduling of Friendly Visitors.

3) **Recording Secretary:**
    a) To take minutes at all core group meetings and volunteer meetings.
    b) To send out copies of minutes to core group and volunteers.
    c) To notify all volunteers and core group of upcoming events and meetings.
    d) To work closely with the coordinators and liaison of program in coordinating correspondence.

Volunteer Job Description
Ministry of Transportation

Purpose of Ministry:

To provide transportation to doctor/dentist appointments, shopping, and weekend liturgies when no other means of transportation is available

Volunteer's Qualifications:

A dependable driver with access to a car and some familiarity with area where transportation is needed

Responsibilities of Volunteer:

To be certain of correct information concerning name of person needing transportation, address, time, telephone number

To be prompt

To contact chairperson in as much advance time as possible if unable to keep the appointment

To notify chairperson of changes in specific day(s)/time(s) of availability

To complete monthly report for chairperson

CASA Volunteer Job Description

Title: **Food Pantry Attendant**
Purpose:
1) To make fair and equitable food distribution judgments.
2) To take and file information from clients at the time food is distributed.

Qualifications:
1) Basically we need people who are good listeners, non-judgmental, sympathetic, understanding, assertive and who have a willingness to help others.

Responsibilities:
1) Conduct interview with client.
2) Assess client's eligibility.
3) Make plans for follow-up (with coordinator).
4) Select and distribute food.
5) To help build a cooperative spirit with volunteers.

Our Responsibility To You:
1) TRAINING: we will provide you with the necessary training and orientation to work in the Food Pantry. This four-part program will be on four consecutive Tuesday evenings in English and on four consecutive Sundays in Spanish.

Commitment:
   All we ask is that you pledge to work one three-hour shift per month on either a Wednesday or a Saturday and that you attend and participate in periodic volunteer meetings.

Title: **Friendly Visitor**
Purpose:
1) To show interest in and concern for the homebound.
2) To demonstrate the caring attitude of the parish.

Qualifications:
1) Basically we are looking for people who are open-minded about the unique qualities of people and dependable. You should also be a good listener, a good observer and able to laugh.

Responsibilities:
1) To visit and converse with a homebound person once a week.
2) To play games or other recreational activities with the person (e.g. play cards or checkers).
3) To establish a relationship with the person.
4) However we do not do chores for the people.

Our Responsibility To You:
1) TRAINING: we will provide the same types of orientation as we do for food pantry workers. (For details see food pantry training).

Commitment:
1) You will be asked to visit each client once a week.
2) You will be asked to fill out a monthly log of your visits. You will be shown how to do this in the training sessions.
3) You are asked to attend periodic volunteer meetings.

   We ask that if you do join us you make a two-month commitment to try it out and then if you like it you may commit yourself for six months or a year. . . .Of course once you do get involved in the program you may always change your assignment or adjust your schedule. Why not come and give it a try? There are many people waiting for you to care and share.

Volunteer Application

Name _____

Address _____

Phone: Day _____ Evening _____

Number of other persons in home _____ Foreign language spoken _____

Do you own a car? _____ Have a valid driver's license? _____

Hobbies, Skills, Special Interest/Training_____

_____

List previous volunteer experiences _____

_____

Other community affiliations _____

If presently employed, occupation_____

Employer _____

Briefly describe responsibilities _____

Type of volunteer work interested in: _____ Food Pantry Worker
                                        _____ Friendly Visitor
                                        _____ Other

If possible check times available:

	AM	PM	Evening
Sunday			
Monday			
Tuesday			
Wednesday			
Thursday			
Friday			
Saturday			

How many days per week? _____ How many hours per week? _____

How did you hear about our program? _____

Why do you wish to volunteer? _____

_____

Are there any medical or other limitations on type of work you can do?_____

_____

Person to notify in case of emergency:

Name _____

Address_____

Phone _____ Date of Application _____

Your Signature_____

122

PART III:

Processes of Parish Social Ministry

Woman Weeping

SIX

Social Action

Social action has a long history in America, beginning with this country's very foundations. Throughout this history, many groups with a myriad of causes have employed social action tactics to influence social change.

The American parish has engaged in social actions as a legitimate methodology to express its ministry and to act on its values. Examples of social action at the parish level span a wide variety of issues, from abortion protest to nuclear freeze.

Most instances of parish social action relate to local issues, as for example, an incident in East Toledo, Ohio where parishioners organized and checked out all the books from the neighborhood library when the city decided to close it. The library remained open. Another self-help social action story involves parishes countering the actions of realtors in an East Coast city who began blockbusting in a middle class neighborhood. Long-time parish residents soon organized and joined with other church and civic groups to stop the practice. In these instances, the churches and community groups successfully organized to change institutional policies. (*The Ethnic Response: Parish/Neighborhood Survival*, 16m film, Peeler Productions).

Parishioners have even utilized social action within the Church itself. Ethnic Catholics in the early decades of this century engaged in social action when they built their own churches and imported pastors who spoke their language (sometimes in direct opposition to Church authorities). In later years, parishes employed social action by joining forces with the labor movement to bring about more humane working conditions and better wages.

The issues may vary, but social action as an effective tool of parish social ministry remains solidly ingrained in the character of the American parish.

Social action has taken on many causes. Justice is its motivating force. It aims to improve services, effect change in public policy or social structure through group action. By its nature, social action pertains to communal values and communal activity. Recent Church social teachings urge transformation and renewal of the social order and further legitimatize social action as a valid means for parishioners to use to respond to their baptismal call. Catholic Charities, in its renewal efforts, includes humanizing and transforming the social order as one of its three major functions. Parish social ministry under Catholic Charities' auspices rightly emphasizes social action.

A subsequent chapter will touch on combining social action with direct service. Discussion here centers on social action itself, including a quick overview of several major social action methodologies.

SOCIAL ACTION METHODS

Just as skills are needed to effectively provide direct services such as counseling or organizing a food pantry, skills are also important in acting for justice. Throughout our history, groups engaged in social action have developed various sets of strategies which have consistently proved effective in achieving their objectives and thus, over time, have developed into conventional methodologies. These include: boycotts, peaceful protest, legislative advocacy, community organizing, community development, alternate economic systems, resistance, and even civil disobedience.

They comprise the more celebrated social action methods used to bring about social change. Depending on specific circumstances or issues being addressed, each can be employed effectively at an appropriate stage of social change. In the context of parish social ministry, these methodologies also aim to develop community.

Peaceful Protest

Peaceful protest, such as demonstrations, primarily serves to bring wide public attention to a national or international issue such as nuclear war, apartheid, abortion. Peaceful protest calls attention to a basic injustice and attempts to gain public support and garner favorable public opinion for the cause. Examples of peaceful protest were common in the 1960's during the civil rights struggle. In more recent times, parishes have also utilized protest as a form of social action. Parishes have joined demonstrators to protest nuclear war, abortion, and the apartheid policies of the government of South Africa.

The moral strength of peaceful protest stems from its total reliance on non-violence as a tactic, even in the face of danger and bodily harm. Violence by the protestors nullifies this moral power. Violence may also reduce public support as well as cloud the main issue because of unfavorable controversy that diverts attention from the issue to the tactic. (Such has been the case with the Pittsburgh ministers, who protesting industrial policies, diverted public attention from the issue to themselves when they intimidated families of the company executives; also, the bombings of abortion clinics and violence against civilians in Northern Ireland are other instances in which attention is diverted from the issue to the tactic).

However, peaceful protest remains a very legitimate form of social action which can effectively gain wide public support. When coupled with other forms of social action, its effectiveness increases.

Resistance

Resistance expresses a highly sophisticated form of social protest which may, though not necessarily, include civil disobedience or sabotage. It is usually employed in extreme situations such as war or subjugation. It aims at significant structural change by undermining production or interfering with the authority's course of action. Success depends on mass adherence to the tactics. Recent international events have called attention to resistance as a form of protest in parishes both here and abroad. Resistance fighters are aware of what the consequences of their actions may bring, as witnessed by the indictment of members of the Sanctuary movement in the United States; the torture and death of Solidarnosc supporters, such as Father Popieluszko in Poland; and the murder of Archbishop Oscar Romero of San Salvador.

An example of resistance closer to home concerns members of a parish community in Mobile, AL who withheld the taxes on their long distance phone bills. These taxes had been levied by Congress to support the Vietnam war and later, war materials. The phone company reported the members of the community to the Internal Revenue Service. Some members then had their salaries garnisheed until payment was made. Their taxes were then audited each year. Another eventually paid the tax—in pennies. Although forced to comply, their resistance tactics nonetheless sent a message to the authorities.

Boycott

A boycott aims at the economic jugular. It is a means of coercion. To boycott means to refuse to buy or use a certain product or service from a company or organization believed to be employing unjust practices. To be effective, the boycott must gain widespread support so that the offending party takes note of declining profits or a negative public image. Those boycotting must be willing to do without the product or services for an extended period of time. Recent examples include: the grape and lettuce boycott in support of the California farm workers' right to unionize; the Nestle boycott to protest that company's international baby food policy of selling baby formula to Third World countries, which, given the situation in these countries, was detrimental; and the Campbell Soup Company boycott in support of farmworkers' right to self-determination and to enter into crop contract negotiations between the growers and the processors.

Parishes have also used the boycott locally as a strategy to change local institutional policy. For example, in one major city, a number of urban parishes employed a type of boycott against local banks. The parishes aimed to change banking practices that were detrimental to neighborhood vitality, particularly the banks' refusal to provide loans for home repair in a certain section of the the city which the banks arbitrarily redlined. The parishes joined with other groups and successfully boycotted banks that were redlining particular neighborhoods. By withdrawing their savings and closing their bank accounts, parishioners and other local residents changed the bank's redlining practice.

The boycott strategy demands considerable planning, education, organizing, and discipline. Boycott organizers must have reasonable surety that they will be able to gain sufficient support to make an economic difference. At the same time, negotiating skills are necessary to discuss the reasons for the boycott with the offending company officials and to obtain commitments for policy change.

Legislative Advocacy

Initiating legislative action, or advocating on behalf of legislation at the local, state and national levels expresses a familiar type of social action developed in parish social ministry. Frequently the parish joins other groups or organizations who support the issue. Examples include, at the local level, parishioners contacting city or county representatives to introduce restrictive zoning legislation such as disallowing bars near playgrounds; or at the state level, lobbying with others to obtain tax relief for elderly homeowners; and on the national level, lobbying congressional representatives to support housing legislation for the poor.

Community Organizing

Organizing, as an effective method of social action, is as American as apple pie, and older than the Constitution. One of the earliest accounts of its applications dates back to the settlement of Virginia when Polish glass workers were denied voting rights. The workers organized, and withheld their services until they received the same rights as the English settlers.

Organizing, as used below, refers to the Alinsky method of mass organization for power; that is, enough people with similar interests getting together so they create power to change situations more in their favor. (Alinsky, S.D. *Rules for Radicals*, p. 114).

During the formative years of the labor movement in this country, labor leaders vigorously employed organizing tactics to build the labor organization. Again in the 1960's and 1970's, neighborhood and community groups used community organizing techniques to pressure local governments or other authorities to improve or establish basic services such as sanitation, safety, housing, health facilities, etc. Highly trained organizers worked with community groups to develop local leadership, target issues and plan action to effect change in favor of the organized group.

Some parishes have adopted community organizing techniques, with and without modification. For greater effectiveness, parishes have joined with other churches and organizations in broad-based community organizing activities which address a wide variety of issues such as Medicaid legislation, rent control, and housing developments.

Church-related community organizations have recognized the value of including reflection on Gospel values in the organizing process. **The parish community-building process (discussed later) employs many community organizing techniques, but with the major emphasis on community, prayer, reflection, and inculcation of religious values, particularly the basic tenet of respect for human dignity.**

130

Alternative Action

Alternative action aims to establish a competing system or institution as an option that offers greater benefits than the established system. One example is parish credit unions, which may function as an alternative economic system as well as a banking institution, sometimes the only one in which poor people can participate. Other examples include cooperatives, including food, housing, and farming cooperatives. Some parishes promote the alternative Christmas to counter the commercialism of that holiday.

Examples of Parish Social Action

The following examples indicate how some parishes and Catholic Charities agencies have utilized social action in their parish social ministry efforts. Discussion centers on legislative advocacy, community organizing, alternative systems, community development, and institutional change, which are the more frequent applications of social action at the parish level.

Legislative Advocacy

Parish Representatives on Diocesan Teams: Baltimore's LEG

In Baltimore, Catholic Charities has established a special legislative thrust with its Legislative Education Group (LEG). LEG aims to involve parishioners in the agency's legislative advocacy efforts at the state level. When Catholic Charities supported a foster care bill in the state General Assembly, it approached the parishes for assistance.

Charities social concerns staff talked with pastors, parish councils, and parish community relations committees about the foster care legislation with the hope of recruiting at least one representative from each parish to act as a LEG contact person. As the LEG contact, the parish volunteer recruits other parishioners to write or call the state legislators about the bill. The contacts stay informed through a newsletter and background materials such as a copy of the bill, a list of legislators and information about the state's General Assembly. Parishes were organized by legislative districts, with a coordinator for each district who served as liaison between the agency and the parish contacts.

This first attempt at parish legislative advocacy proved successful, as the bill passed. The LEG network expanded to other agency-supported legislation on housing, welfare, energy, children, and the handicapped. The expansion did not work so well and the agency restructured its approach to allow parish volunteers to choose to work for any of the agency legislative priorities rather than restrict themselves to issues determined by the agency. The agency also initiated better communications through an improved newsletter, publicity, and public forums. Although the agency staff encourages parish convenings on the issues, volunteer initiated convenings are uncommon. However, the agency staff believe that LEG's success stems from the fact that they do not preach social justice, but that the parishioners learn about people in need and how to become involved in changing the system.

This particular approach to introducing social action at the parish level has merit, as the Baltimore experience demonstrates. The LEG experience illustrates some of the principles of parish social ministry, particularly those of empowering the parish to leadership; transcending parochial and provincial issues; addressing social and community needs through service and action; and fostering a preferential option for the poor. However, because of its strong emphasis on issues, it engages less vigorously in nurturing the baptismal call to ministry, building community, and allowing for sufficient self-determination and ownership of the issues within the parishes. With some slight modification, the Baltimore approach has considerable potential as a model for other agencies seeking ways to inculcate social action in parish social ministry.

Networking Parishes for Social Change: Seattle

Seattle Catholic Charities also conducts legislative social action that bears some similarities to the Baltimore program, but Seattle places greater emphasis on networking parishes. "We try to educate parishioners on the need for social programs and what legislation is being enacted. Our focus is the parish. We try to educate, inform, reflect and act," said Tony Lee, a legislative liaison for Catholic Charities Justice and Peace Center.

In King County, Catholic Community Services set up a legislative network of 10 to 15 parishes. Mr. Lee also works with about seven parishes in another county, giving workshops and coordinating legislative work with the parishes and other community groups. Plans include setting up parish networks in all six regions of the diocese.

Recently Mr. Lee worked with 11 inner city parishes regarding the severe housing shortage for low income persons. "We're coordinating efforts of several parishes, including St. Joseph's, St. Paul's, St. Patrick's, and St. James, by setting up a social justice coordinating committee. Parishes working by themselves are less effective. Networking breaks down the sense of isolation that parishes sometimes feel and it increases their resources," he said. These inner city parishes along with low income groups are pushing for anti-abandonment legislation. Mr. Lee explained that some building owners abandon their buildings and hold them to sell to speculators.

Other issues that parishioners have lobbied, called, and written about to state legislators concern adequate income for the poor, including restoration of AFDC programs and an increase in public assistance grants.

Alternate Economic System

Parish Credit Unions in Imperial Valley

In the Imperial Valley of California in the early 1980's, survival was the name of the game. Unemployment climbed in the Hispanic community, reaching eventually 40 percent. Poverty, at a 30 percent rate, was almost as rampant. Mechanization started to replace the need for unskilled and uneducated agricultural workers. Many laborers were locked out of the economic system, unable to obtain credit. The only hope came from a substitute economic system.

As the economic situation worsened, Catholic Charities responded with a new approach: reach the people through the parishes, said John Graykoski, who headed Imperial Valley Catholic Community Services at that time.

"The parishes were untouched for years," Mr. Graykoski said, "in an area of about 100,000 people, 70 percent of whom were Catholic. There was little commitment to the Church, and it was difficult to motivate people." The initial approach aimed at parish renewal, a conversion process which would eventually impact on the community, he explained.

133

Effects of Unemployment
Worse for this Recession
1. Rates are Higher than any time since 194[
2. The recession is of Long Duration
3. No national vision or Plan for Retraining
4. More Structural Unemployment

Through the parishes, "we were trying to make an impact through structural change." After a two-year convening process, the agency assisted nine parishes in their first project: a community development credit union to build an economic system.

The credit union became a vehicle to "capture money that was flowing out of the Valley for use here where it belongs," Mr. Graykoski added. "The member-owners of the credit union listen, identify and prioritize the needs of the community. They then direct their pooled capital to investments which will directly impact on the areas of need," he said.

The credit union allowed the people "to control the financial portion of their lives," said Dan Lackey who headed the credit union project in its formative stages. "The credit unions were chartered to serve the members of the parishes," he said.

"The members operate the credit union," Mr. Lackey added. Parish volunteers were trained to promote the credit union, take loan applications, and sign up new members.

134

A grant from the Southwest Border Regional Commission allowed the credit union to hire a professional manager. Income from the credit union members, parish donations and eight religious communities, helped build assets.

After five difficult years of struggle, the credit union assets have steadily grown to over $350,000. "We're slowly growing. Our rating is up, we're doing better," said Rey Bracamonte, current director, who began as a parish volunteer. "We've helped a lot of people. We've loaned out $585,000 since we've formed. We have a lot of low income agricultural workers, people who couldn't get bank loans. We've helped young adults get started. I see a good future for our credit union," he added.

In addition to the parish-based credit unions, Catholic Charities attempted to bring about change through other means. It assisted with programs for drug abuse, delinquency, job training, housing and a food cooperative. According to Mr. Graykoski, the role of the agency developed "to lend organizational and administrative support to grassroots efforts of community improvement. The impetus to improve communities and find solutions to problems should come from the residents of those communities rather than emanate from a social service agency," he said.

Institutional Change

St. Richard's Parish, Minneapolis, MN

Attempts to bring about change through parish social ministry do not always approach a scale as large and challenging as that in Imperial Valley. St. Richards' Parish in Minneapolis illustrates changes brought about in one institution through organized parish action.

St. Richard's parish boundaries encompass five retirement centers which parish volunteers visit weekly. During visits at one center, parishioners noticed that the people were often sick, listless, and complained of their food. The parish visitors encountered this situation so frequently that they decided to investigate.

"We prepared a strategy, how to go about it, what was it that needed change, and where was the problem," said Sister Mary Zirbes, director of Parish Social Ministry, Catholic Charities of the Archdiocese of St. Paul and Minneapolis.

The first action consisted of investigating the problem to verify and substantiate the visitors' impressions. A group of parish visitors interviewed as many of the retirees as possible, but they found it difficult to get the residents to respond. "They were very afraid of management. They'd said that if the management found out they complained or said anything that wasn't positive about the institution, they would be threatened or sent out onto the street," said Sister Zirbes.

To overcome this difficulty, the parish visitors who had very good relationships with the retirees did the investigating. "What was said was kept very confidential. What we heard over and over was that these people were not getting their prescribed diets. (In addition) there was no check system. On separated occasions, two individuals had broken their leg and had been lying there for a half day before they'd been found. This was critical."

Further investigation revealed that there was no dietitian. "We went to talk to the administrator about it, but there was no change over a period of time."

The next step the social ministers took involved organizing 30 elderly people from the parish community as potential candidates for the center. "We prepared them for an evening of confrontation with the administrator since no change had been made. We took our 30 elderly people as well as our committee, and three spokespersons. Everyone was well prepared. We presented our case. We wanted a check system so that people would be found immediately if they weren't around or didn't show up," Sister Zirbes explained. They also asked for a dietitian to prepare proper meals.

"Those were our two requests. We presented our case to the administrator who was obviously extremely nervous. Finally we got him to listen, but got no firm promise from him. We left the meeting and organized a follow-up meeting of five people to meet with the administrator. We continued putting the pressure on. Eventually we were successful. We got a dietitian in there several days a week and we got a check system that the people felt could be helpful to them.

"The relationship between that institution and the parish became much stronger because that administrator knew that we were concerned about the people, and he did want us to continue to visit. But he was also aware that we were concerned that the institution remain there and remain an effective institution," she concluded.

St. Richard's experience illustrates how institutional policy changes and improved services can result from social action taken by one parish. Some of the elements of the social action process the parish utilized are worth noting. First, the action stemmed from a service that the parish provided, namely visitation of institutionalized elderly. Secondly, questionable conditions experienced by the elderly were carefully investigated. **The parish visitors documented their case. Next, the social ministers planned a step-by-step strategy with persistent follow-up. They did not give up as long as the conditions they wanted to change continued. Finally, came change and reconciliation.** The victory that the parish social ministers gained was not so much a vindication as it was a nurturing and renewal of their relationship with the institution.

Community Development

St. Paul's Parish, Bloomingdale, N.Y.

St. Paul's parish, located in a **small rural community** of about 500 people near the Saranac Valley in the Adirondacks, illustrates ecumenical social action to bring a needed service to the general community.

Bloomingdale, like many small towns, experienced a shortage of adequate housing for the elderly. St. Paul's pastor, Father Peter Ward, learned of technical housing assistance available from the Ogdensburg diocese Catholic Charities and invited Father Stephen Gratto from the agency to speak at a town meeting, organized by St. Paul's, to discuss the possibility of a senior housing project for the village.

"Father Steve spoke to an old-fashioned town meeting, a group of a very fine cross section of our population. From that came a steering committee and a not-for-profit corporation called Senior Citizens Overlook Inc.," Father Ward explained.

One of the problems that the group had to overcome related to the small size of the village. A village with a population of only 500 could very easily be dismissed by government bureaucracy. **The people had to learn to trust the power of their organized efforts. St. Paul's parish, with assistance from Catholic Charities, played the role of catalyst in the community** by bringing together a cross section of community members and not only presenting the possiblity of housing for the elderly in the area, but inspiring the community to take action.

Within two years of that town meeting, Bloomingdale had 20 units of senior citizen housing under construction. The citizens' corporation, comprised of members of the parish, civic organizations and other churches, worked with Catholic Charities housing expert, Alex Velto, to complete the necessary studies and file the mounds of paperwork to obtain a $500,000 government loan for housing.

"People from all walks of life and all ages have done their part in making it possible," Father Ward said. "Not only those living there, but everyone in the village is proud of what has been accomplished by a good many people doing a little bit here, a little bit there."

This example illustrates two desirable aspects of social action ministry: ecumenical cooperation and development of the community. The parish clearly saw itself as an active partner in the broader community as well as a service leader in that community. **The parish placed high priority on its service role. The pastor also played a key part by enthusiastically supporting parish participation in the project and by his willingness to utilize Catholic Charities' resources and technical assistance.**

Convening for Self-Help

St. Teresa's Parish, Kankakee, IL

St. Teresa's story bears some similarities to that of St. Paul's, particulary in regard to the parish joining with others to transcend parochial issues and its utilizing Catholic Charities as a technical resource.

The parish, located in an economically depressed and high unemployment area of Kankakee, IL, in the Joliet diocese, asked Catholic Charities and the diocesan Social Concerns Office to help the parish develop social ministry that would respond to the needs brought about by the economic conditions.

First, the parish formed a planning group which embarked on an empowerment process for the parish to respond to community needs and to join with other community groups to meet these needs.

The parish sponsored a town hall gathering, issuing invitations to Kankakee city leaders. Positive response resulted in participation of representatives from the Salvation Army, Rehabilitation Services, the Community Action Agency, Job Services, Kankakee College, as well as parishioners, community residents and community leaders such as the alderman and city planner.

From the discussion emerged a parish commitment to develop ministries to respond to the most prevalent needs, including emergency services and shelter for the homeless.

"It's the Church in the marketplace," said St. Teresa pastor, Father Joel Fortier. "This process took our parishioners beyond our parochial concerns to the larger community. They feel valued by the broader leadership in the community, and are eager to take ownership of the concerns."

Community Organizing

St. Pius X Parish and Houma Indians Organize

St. Pius parish, in the Louisiana bayous, called in Catholic Charities parish social ministry to assist an Indian group, the Houmas, which comprised almost 75 percent of the parish population. The Houmas faced several problems, including a high incidence of poverty, lack of federal recognition, high unemployment, and loss of their culture, explained Mary

Baudouin, parish social ministry director at Associated Catholic Charities of New Orleans.

Moreover, the state legislation was considering dropping the Governor's Commission on Indian Affairs from the state budget which would eliminate such government assistance to the tribe as higher education grants, energy assistance, weatherization programs, and summer camps.

In response to a request by Father Richard Maughan, pastor of Pius X, Ms. Baudouin, along with Charities organizer, Jeff Conner, and attorney Bill Quigley attended a meeting of the United Houma Nation Tribal Council. The Council seemed to lack the needed skills to organize the tribe to rally around a specific issue, Ms. Baudouin observed. The Charities organizer helped the tribe develop its leadership skills and focus on the immediate impending loss of state programs.

The tribe resolved to go to Baton Rouge to lobby state senators and representatives on the budget committee. Charities also obtained the help of the assistant director of the Office of Indian Affairs to help the tribe develop a lobbying strategy. A week later, 40 Houmas set off to Baton Rouge. On the front steps of the state capitol they formed a large circle and sang the Lord's Prayer in traditional Indian chant. "The group then entered the capitol and individually lobbied state senators and representatives before going into the budget committee hearing," Ms. Baudouin reports. The tribe's lobbying efforts proved so effective that the budget committee never even raised the question of eliminating the Commission on Indian Affairs from the state budget!

In savoring their first taste of victory, the Houmas regained their confidence and began to focus their energies on other issues, including an amended budget to increase state funds for Indian programs; an Indian festival to celebrate their heritage and culture; and a petition to the federal government for recognition as a nation.

"St. Pius X parish is looking towards the future," Ms. Baudouin said. "The parish is using the community building process and identifying other community issues. We at the Parish Social Ministry office feel privileged to have such a unique and enriching opportunity to work with the Houmas."

Ecumenical Community Organizing in Washington, D.C.

Most social action advocates would agree that social action which is broad-based is more effective than if reserved to the parish itself. (Although there may be times when the parish must take on an issue alone). In the late 1970's Associated Catholic Charities of the Washington Archdiocese helped sponsor a self-help community action organization consisting of 10 Catholic parishes and 28 Protestant churches. The ecumenically-sponsored organization, Project WISH (Washington Inner-city Self Help) aimed to involve neighborhood people to seek solutions to their problems. According to Father Carl Dianda, who was pastor at St. Martin's parish, WISH tried to "revitalize and rebuild community."

Each church contributed money, equipment, or space which, along with a grant from the Campaign for Human Development, provided the support for the project.

According to Rev. Don Leaming-Elmer, who was WISH project director, the most difficult aspect of the project was to motivate people to act, a majority of whom were "extremely poor," he stated.

Issues concerning the neighborhood residents included crime, transportation, garbage collection, and housing. Some of the changes that organized social action brought about included: repair of broken mailboxes, repaired furnaces, installation of security systems, return of illegal and excessive rent payment, and rehabilitation of buildings to conform to code standards.

"Our initial victories have broken through a lot of the hopelessness of the people we work with. Getting the garbage picked up and getting the

landlord to fix up your apartment is a significant step in gaining control of your life," he said.

The WISH project is a classic community organizing process that many urban parishes experienced during the 1970's. The characteristics of this type of social action include: **formation of a coalition**—in this case, a rather large ecumenical group of 38 **churches—to sponsor and fund the action; hiring of a professional organizer; organizing clusters of neighborhood people; and focus on immediate neighborhood issues that are within reach of resolution**, the completion of which provides the group with a sense of its power and identity.

GROWTH THROUGH EXPERIENCE

One limitation of some past church-sponsored community organizing and other social action efforts was that it created an impression that parishioners were removed from social ministry. The parish became *institutionally* involved and the clergy were personally committed to social justice, but parishioners often were not directly involved nor committed to either the process or the issues. Sometimes, misunderstanding or divisiveness occurred within the parish, especially between pastor and flock. Recognition of this shortcoming by organizing practitioners within Catholic Charities has led to closer analysis of the nature of parish social ministry, with renewed emphasis on Gospel values, educating parishioners on Church social teachings, and the building of community through social ministry.

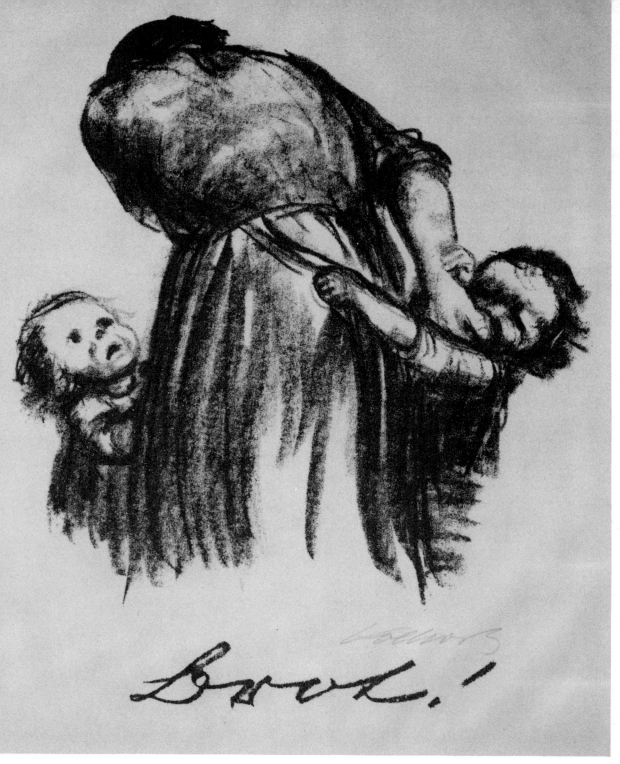

144   *Bread!*

SEVEN

Direct Service

On July 26, 1979, Xuan Phan and four Vietnamese children, survivors of the Boat People crisis, arrived in St. Paul, Minnesota. Two of the children, Hein, 14, and HaiDang, 18 months old, had been orphaned in their boat escape. At the refugee camp in Malaysia, alone and frightened, Xuan began to care for them. She became their source of strength as this newly-formed family made its journey to the United States and eventually to Guardian Angels parish in Lake Elmo, Minnesota, which sponsored their resettlement.

"We thanked God for this family's safe arrival and set about the task of helping them build a future," said Judy Scheider, one of the parishioners involved in the parish refugee resettlement program. (*Promises of Hope*, Archdiocese of St. Paul and Minneapolis).

So begins the story of one parish's experiences in social ministry. Many parishes throughout the country can relate similar stories. Refugee resettlement exemplifies one of the more dramatic expressions of service ministry.

Direct service, in which parishioners *individually* volunteer time and effort to help others, expresses a familiar type of parish social ministry. Direct service ministry spans a wide range of activities—from emergency food, friendly visitors, telephone assurance, home assistance and chore service, transportation and shopping helpers, respite care, hospital visitation, bereavement support, legal aid, child care, tutors, referral services, clothing shops, to whatever else parishes see as an immediate need in their communities.

Sometimes the parish offers several types of services independently of each other or as part of a package of social ministry activities. We'll examine some examples of the direct service ministry in parishes in several dioceses.

145

STRUCTURED MINISTRY:

Chicago Archdiocese

Chicago Catholic Charities Parish Social Ministry, under the direction of Sister Shirley Fineran, conducts one of the largest parish social ministry efforts in the country, much of it related to direct services. The two parishes described here have developed highly structured service ministry with Catholic Charities assistance. These parishes have incorporated service ministry into the parish, given it high visibility, and made it a major part of parish life. Catholic Charities Parish-Community Services provides consultation and training to the parishes through a regional coordinator and/or trainer for volunteers.

Specifying Ministry:
Our Lady of Mt. Carmel Church, Melrose Park, IL

Our Lady of Mt. Carmel initiated Caring and Sharing Action (CASA) which serves Italian-, Spanish-, and English-speaking members of the parish/community. CASA services include friendly visiting and an emergency food pantry.

The parish's social ministry effort is well defined. Guidelines exist for friendly visiting, spelling out expectations of the parish visitor in terms of what a visitor does, how often and how long visitations should take, what may be accomplished, reporting procedures, and who will benefit from the service. Similar guidelines exist for the food pantry service.

Each service—the food pantry, friendly visiting, and Spanish-speaking volunteers—has a team of parish coordinators, who along with a pastor and secretary comprise a core group. Roles are clearly defined. Each member of the core group has a set of written responsibilities so all know what is expected of one another.

CASA places considerable emphasis on the parish volunteer. Parishioners are recruited through a volunteer recruitment form and volunteers are screened through an application process. In addition, job descriptions containing the title, purpose, qualifications, responsibilities and commitment, are written for all volunteers such as the food pantry attendant, and friendly visitor. Volunteers, trained in their respective job tasks, have specific procedures to follow.*

The CASA services are striking in their organization and structure, which immediately imbues a sense of dignity, stability and permanence to the service. The procedures CASA follows assure that uniformity, consistency, and quality are built into the parish's service ministry.

What does this tell the person in need? First, that considerable time and effort were invested in his/her needs, and secondly, their needs are taken very seriously. Those who receive service know that if they come back tomorrow, someone will be there to help. These characteristics send an important message to the vulnerable, whose lives frequently lack a sense of stability and worth.

Divine Providence, Westchester IL

A similar service ministry program exists at Divine Providence parish. Services there include caring visitors, youth home maintenance for seniors, and transportation and errands. The parish has a ministry coor-

---

See Appendix C, Chapter Three for samples of CASA guidelines, responsibilities, volunteer job descriptions, recruitment form, volunteer application, food pantry schedule, food intake form, and friendly visitor record form.

dinator and chairpersons for the services. A parish deacon serves as liaison. Again, **job descriptions exist for all core members and volunteers**.

Social ministry at these two parishes is highly structured on a social service model, reflecting the influence of Catholic Charities service experience.

*Training and Resource Development: Honolulu**

Parish service ministry in this diocese offers a good example of an agency utilizing the networking concept. Since 1977, 13 parishes have initiated service ministry, each marking its ministry with the distinct gifts of the parish. **The process used in most of the parishes consists of assessing the parish/community needs and resources; providing opportunities to serve; and involving and empowering people**.

Each parish provides basic services such as food or financial help, and adds services to meet the specific needs of its community. Some of these services include:

Hospice: seven parishes have trained 125 volunteers through a hospital hospice program so that parishioners may give supportive care to terminally ill patients and their families. The volunteers work in conjunction with a hospital team.

Bereavement: several parishes provide bereavement packets to parishioners who have lost a loved one. Some offer one-to-one support to the bereaved person. Another parish gives monthly talks on death and dying.

Welcome: several parishes greet new parishioners with a lei during Sunday Mass; after services, newcomers meet parishioners over coffee and donuts. Later they may receive a welcoming letter or visit.

Food Pantry: parishes collect food items or use a food bank for food distribution. A few may concentrate on distributing food baskets at holidays.

Friendly visits: parishioners visit the sick, invalid or elderly.

Other: healing and annointing service; babysitting; homework helpers.

---

* The Honolulu diocese is currently restructuring with renewed emphasis on the parish social ministry. See Chapter 3, Integrating Parish Social Ministry within the Catholic Charities Agency.

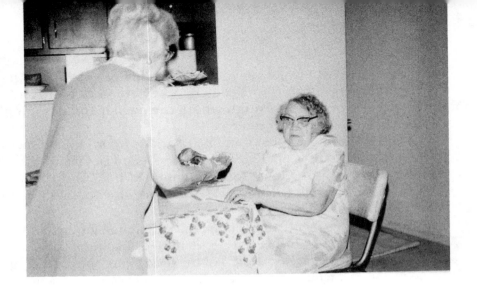

Catholic Charities Parish Outreach coordinator provides consultation, training, and resource development to the parishes. **One of the methods used by the agency coordinator involves a workshop on a particular ministry.** For example 11 parishes attended a Growth through Grief workshop, from which four parishes set up bereavement outreach. Similar results were obtained after a hospice presentation.

The Honolulu experience stresses the network approach to service ministry which proves significant in areas with limited resources.

Tapping Resources and Networking: Manchester, N.H.

The Manchester diocese encompasses the whole state of New Hampshire. As such, the agency faces many of the challenges characteristic of both urban and rural areas in supporting parish social ministry, including great travel distances, isolation, and limited resources. The service ministry here, although similar in many ways to that of other dioceses, displays some unique aspects.

More House Project

This service ministry provides a unique ministry in the Manchester diocese. More House is a Catholic Charities-operated, parish-sponsored, summer ministry for urban and rural areas. Although it operates in the summer, it is part of a larger, on-going community process in which student lay ministers offer service to others. **A key element of this ministry involves a process through which the parish and community define their goals and concerns**.

In a letter of application to Catholic Charities from Virginia Lewis of the Community Affairs Committee and Father Gerard Desmarais, associate pastor, to sponsor More House for the summer of 1985, the parish community of St. Joseph in Laconia, N.H. explained its expectations of the summer ministry.

Through dialogue with other community churches, groups, and agencies, six general areas of need were identified, including an outreach program for the elderly; expansion of the food pantry program; organization of a soup kitchen; youth counseling (drop-in center); establishment of an emergency assistance coordination program with mutual referrals between the churches and human services agencies; advocacy for low income people; and determination of shelter and housing needs in the area.

Other churches and local agencies participating in the assessments include Sacred Heart parish, St. James Episcopal, Good Shepherd Lutheran, Congregational Church of Laconia, and community agencies and service organizations.

Past More House ministries included a survey of agricultural land use; a needs assessment of homebound elderly; establishment of a community food pantry; a feasibility survey of mobil home solarization; and a study of alternative uses of church facilities.

According to Dick Shannon, director of New Hampshire Catholic Charities Parish Social Ministry, the More House ministry is not a one-time summer project which ends after the students leave. Rather, it allows parishes to tap additional resources in their ongoing social ministry or provides a resource to help the parish community initiate a service ministry. **Many of the components of the social ministry process are evident: pastor and parish leadership support; discerning needs and resources; planning; goal setting; and networking with other parishes and community groups**.

Faith Revealed through Service: St. John the Baptist, Manchester, N.H.

St. John's is a primarily ethnic parish community of 1200 French-Canadian families in West Manchester. The parish, under the leadership of Father Paul Gregoile, the pastor, completed the RENEW process in 1984 which motivated a number of parishioners to seek out ways to more fully live their faith. Two parishioners, Pat and Paul Morin contacted Catholic Charities to help the parish conduct a discernment process to identify community needs and establish priorities. Within six months, Catholic Charities parish outreach staff, Peggy Garvey Mitchell, assisted the parishioners through this process. The parishioners set the goal to establish a food pantry. Fifty volunteers responded.

Still in its early development, the pantry, which assists 100 families a month, currently receives support from nearby parishes.

One of the outgrowths of the food pantry experience has been the realization on the part of the parishioners that they cannot take care of all the hunger needs they encounter. This has led to parishioners advocating on behalf of the hungry. The parish also seeks to involve other churches and parishes in its social ministry endeavors.

St. John's provides a good example of service ministry evolving into other forms of social ministry, in this case, advocacy. **It also illustrates the growth of the parish from that of a parochial community to leadership in the broader social arena**. Several of the steps of the service ministry process are apparent, including the educational and motivational aspect resulting from the RENEW experience, the discernment process of needs and resource assessment, goal setting, action, networking, and development of other ministries.

Matching Needs and Resources: Rockville Centre

St. Mary's, East Islip, N.Y.

Parish social ministry at this parish resulted from a series of needs and opportunities converging at the Parish Outreach Office. It illustrates Catholic Charities pivotal position as a catalyst for parish service ministry.

In the spring of 1982 Parish Outreach received several requests for home health aides. Parish Outreach did not have a home health aide program nor did it have plans for one.

Simultaneously, a number of divorced, separated, and widowed women, along with women seeking to supplement their family income, approached Parish Outreach looking for work.

151

Parish Outreach soon matched the need for home health aides with the women seeking employment. Several months later, a religious sister from the Daughters of Wisdom assigned to the motherhouse located in St. Mary's parish also approached Parish Outreach with a proposal. She explained she had many years experience in home health care as a registered nurse in the inner cities. She volunteered to give professional training to the home health care workers Parish Outreach was matching. Parish Outreach welcomed this professional dimension. The sister recruited other nurse volunteers from the parish who then established a training program. They organized the recruitment and screening of candidates, training sessions, evaluation of patient needs, and the ongoing administration of the program, under the leadership of the Parish Outreach coordinator. Training covers techniques on bathing, dressing, and transferring patients from a bed, preparing meals, and most importantly, just being there with the patient. The patients and the aides determine their work schedules and payment, usually a modest fee. For patients unable to pay or who are ineligible for government assistance, Parish Outreach, in some cases, provides funds to pay for aides.

The program has grown to the point that the parish has recruited 22 volunteer nurses who have trained over 70 aides. Requests to the parish for aides average about 20 each month.

Catholic Charities is considering St. Mary's home health aide program as a model for other parish service ministry programs in the diocese where similar needs exist. This example illustrates the role the agency can play in bringing together divergent needs and resources.

Training Volunteers in Rural Communities: Lubbock, Texas

Mission Church Serves Poor: Sacred Heart/Our Lady of Guadalupe Parish, Plainview

"I had a girl with three children who were staying in the park. I gave them some food. But I had no quilts or blankets to give her. I must get some blankets," said Josefina Vera, who co-chairs the parish social ministry committee at Sacred Heart/Our Lady of Guadalupe parish in Plainview, TX

Guadalupe church, located in a primarily Mexican-American community, is a poor, mission church of Sacred Heart Parish that operates a food pantry as part of its social ministry.

"People come from everywhere. Middle-age families, lots of young mothers, some elderly. We're starting to get people working in the fields. Ladies from the parish help put up food. Some people bring clothes and shoes and we give them out. We have a small room at Guadalupe church," explained Mrs. Vera.

Those who come for the emergency supplies must fill out an application first at Sacred Heart Church. "People come to me. Sometimes I deliver to old people. I give to everyone on an emergency basis. Word got around. I never had to advertise. Usually we have three or four families a day. Sometimes up to 12 or 14 a day. Some come back. We don't want to make it a habit. We give enough food for three or four weeks—rice, beans, macaroni and cheese, cereal, vermicelli—you know, a kind of spaghetti—flour, shortening, bread. We buy about $1000 worth of food from the Food Bank for $200," Mrs. Vera said proudly.

The parish is planning a bake sale to raise funds for the emergency food pantry, which constitutes one of the major parish services. Other services include programs for children and youths, and social events such as talent shows, rodeos, and fund raising events.

Sacred Heart/Guadalupe parish belongs to Catholic Charities parish social ministry network which focuses on charity and justice, direct service and social change, explained Steve Hay, coordinator of Catholic Family Services Justice and Peace Program. Mrs. Vera, along with parish social ministers from parishes in the small towns around Lubbock, TX. attend the diocesan social ministry meetings every three months. "We discuss what has to be done. Some work with teens on drugs. Some do like I do. There are seven different kinds of work we do," she explained. The network supports, informs and trains the parish volunteers in their social ministry efforts, especially important in poor rural communities struggling to live out the Gospel values.

In the above examples, Catholic Charities played a significant role in support of the parish's social ministry efforts. In Chicago, the regional coordinator helped with training and developing guidelines for the service ministry programs. In Honolulu and Lubbock, Charities helped network parishes and provided training. In Rockville Centre, Charities acted as the catalyst through which the various components of the parish program came to realization.

OBSTACLES TO SERVICE MINISTRY

In the next section, the parish social ministry examples illustrate efforts with minimal or no support from Catholic Charities. Most of these service ministries illustrate parishioners' profound hunger for service ministry, even in the face of significant obstacles such as lack of support, structure, know-how, encouragement, affirmation, training, and sometimes resources. The examples presented here show the many problems parishioners encounter in their struggle to live out their call to ministry and attest to parishioners' need to express their ministry. They point out the advantages of an ongoing organized social ministry, and the necessity of integrating social ministry into the total parish structure.

Creative Persistence:
*St. Paul and Minneapolis Archdiocese**

Immaculate Heart of Mary Parish, Minnetonka, Minn.

Immaculate Heart of Mary, sponsor of a resettlement program, demonstrates that social ministry is not always smooth sailing. Parishioner Marilyn Schmit recalls some of the roadblocks and the ways the parishioners overcame them.

"In the mid-70's, our parish, like many others, responded to the plight of Vietnamese refugees. A refugee response committee was formed and they soon committed themselves to sponsoring a single individual," she explained. But one of the problems the committee encountered was the parish council's reluctance to commit an unspecified sum of money. Not to be deterred, the committee creatively solved the dilemma by initiating a special monthly collection called the Matthew 25 Program, which later became a source of income for other projects.

A second problem the committee faced concerned a seeming lack of support from parish leaders. "There have been times when we were frus-

---

*Many of these examples are edited and excerpted from **Promises of Hope**...**stories of peoples journeys living out the beatitudes**, published by Catholic Charities Parish Social Ministry, Archdiocese of St. Paul and Minneapolis, whose permission to quote is gratefully acknowledged.*

trated and angry because the pastor gave pulpit time to a bazaar instead of social action, (and) because we couldn't get announcements in the parish bulletin," Mrs. Schmit noted. Nonetheless, the committee persisted.

Before the program ended we had sponsored five families with a total of 25 members, found dozens of people in our parish who hate meetings but love to help with the work, and made some good friendships. It was estimated that $80,000 worth of labor were donated. We formed job hunting committees, English teaching committees and social committees. We found a spirit of cooperation in our parish. We became more of a community than we had been. (excerpted from *Promises of Hope*. . . , p. 44).

This service ministry story offers several positive lessons. For one, it graphically illustrates some of the harsh realities of parish life. In this case, unenthusiastic support of parish leadership, factors which the committee eventually overcame by creatively tapping parish resources through a second collection and by developing a cooperative spirit among the parishioners.

Determination, persistence, and commitment to service, however, were rewarded with an increased awareness of community and growth of the service ministry into other areas. One wonders if these aspects of parish life could have been further enhanced if social ministry were a permanent feature of parish life, including visible support and affirmation by the total parish.

Finding a Structure for Service: St. Pius X Parish, White Bear Lake, Minn.

St. Pius X has developed a multi-faceted service ministry, including an emergency clothing shelf, emergency food shelf, voter information, marriage counselling referral, a singles support group, and foster grandparents. But it, too, had a fitful start, according to social ministry coordinator, Mary Bosscher.

Back in 1975 organized social ministry at St. Pius X included activities by various women's club guilds. But the social action committee felt that since a parish of 1500 families was so large, a structure of neighborhood groups should begin in order to create little parishes and one-to-one contact. The plan was to divide the parish into four quadrants, and each quadrant into 20 neighborhood groups, with a leader from each neighborhood. A parish worker was hired to carry out the goal of the committee. The idea was great on paper, but never worked well. . . .The neighborhood group program eventually closed down after a three-year trial. (*Promises of Hope*. . . , p. 46).

This story illustrates the dangers of imposing an arbitrary structure on parishioners without involving them in either the process or content of social ministry. When the parish changed its tactics to facilitating involvement in the corporal and spiritual works of mercy, it met with greater success for it addressed immediate, visible needs, to which parishioners were motivated to respond. For instance, to the woman who says, "My husband left and I have no food," an emergency food shelf is able to alleviate the immediate problem. The types of service ministry the parish offers also indicate that some form of a needs assessment, as simple as a request for aid, is an important element of the service ministry process. The more concrete the need, the more specific became the response.

Service ministry at St. Pius X has become a formalized and integral component of parish life. Several other aspects of its service ministry are worth noting. One is that all the service ministry is coordinated by a staff coordinator. This allows for program planning, smooth administration, and parish volunteer support. Secondly, the volunteers are well organized to perform specific tasks, usually at specific hours. There are two types of volunteers. Those who help with needs as they arise, and those who are responsible for a particular program at a specific time. The latter provide about three hours of service a week. They receive training in planning and supervising other volunteers.

Supporting Needs from Afar: St. Jerome Parish, Maplewood, Minn.

Sometimes a parish responds to needs that seem illusive. St. Jerome parish responded to the needs of the Church in other areas of the world with its support for foreign missions. This parish example shows the diversity of parish service ministry and the unique service to which some parishes are called.

During a two-year period, the parish sent over $10,000 to two missions, one in Africa and another in Brazil. It added Appalachia and Jamaica to its mission efforts. What factors helped create such enthusiastic missionary support?

According to parishioner Mary Helmueller, a series of personal involvements may account for this unusual social ministry effort.

Many of us from the Christian Caring Group attended a six-week series on hunger for justice at our parish during Lent. The awareness of the hunger and injustice in Third World countries helped us to decide on an action to follow. We formed St. Jerome Social Action Group and with the help and support of Father Ken Ludescher decided to sponsor a Maryknoll mission in Tanzaria, (*sic*) Africa and an Oblate of Mary Immaculate mission in Recife Brazil because we personally knew the missionaries in these missions. . . . Last year we adopted a new mission in Appalachia. Sister Clarice, our school principal, spent a summer teaching C.C.D. in Jamaica and we supported her work there.

Our funds are extended always through personal contact.

We create an awareness and educate the people by publishing the letters from the missionaries in the church bulletin and have a mission bulletin board at the back of the church. When the missionaries return to the U.S. for a visit, they offer Masses at St. Jerome and thank the people personally. This is so very important.

It was very important to have the strong support of the pastor and it helps to publish letters from the missionaries telling us how the money was used to help our poor brothers and sisters. The personal touch is very important as people want their money to reach the needs of the poor directly.

It has been a lot of fun also. We set up a booth to sell home-canned goods and handiworks at the parish festival and sponsored a dance.

We did not use any strategy or structure to begin. Father Ken just announced it from the pulpit that our parish had decided to sponsor two missions and a second collection would be used to furnish the funds. (*edited and excerpted from Promises of Hope.* . . , pp. 55–56).

158

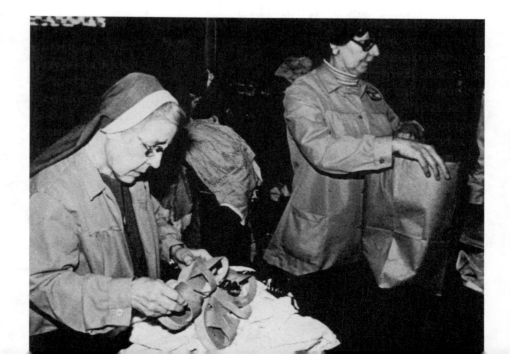

The social activities, amount of money collected, and the number of missions supported indicate a sizeable parish consensus to support the mission ministry.

The parish exemplifies some of the important aspects of the parish social ministry process, including:

- strong support from the pastor;
- an indepth educational and motivational component which led to supporting needs removed from the immediate community;
- a structure (committee) to administer the service;
- involvement of parishioners beyond the original core committee;
- personal knowledge of the missionaries which made a distant need more immediate;
- visible feedback and gratification through the letters and bulletin board;
- a social, fun component and personal commitment of parishioners obtained though the festivals and dances;
- sufficient resources within the parish to support the activities.

ADVANTAGES OF ORGANIZED MINISTRY

Most of the above examples of service ministry illustrate the struggle that many parishes undergo to live out their call to ministry. Several examples point to a major, common difficulty: fragmented or short-lived social ministry because of an ad hoc approach in which success proves erratic and sometimes more painful than need be.

Some parishes may develop successful social ministry because of the personalities involved, the latent desire of many parishioners to activate their call to ministry, or other factors. But, in spite of the success, many parishes may not fully realize that social ministry should become a permanent, ongoing, integral part of parish life. Parish social ministry requires a structure which makes it a permanent feature of parish life. In most instances, Catholic Charities can help the parish develop and build its parish social ministry structures.

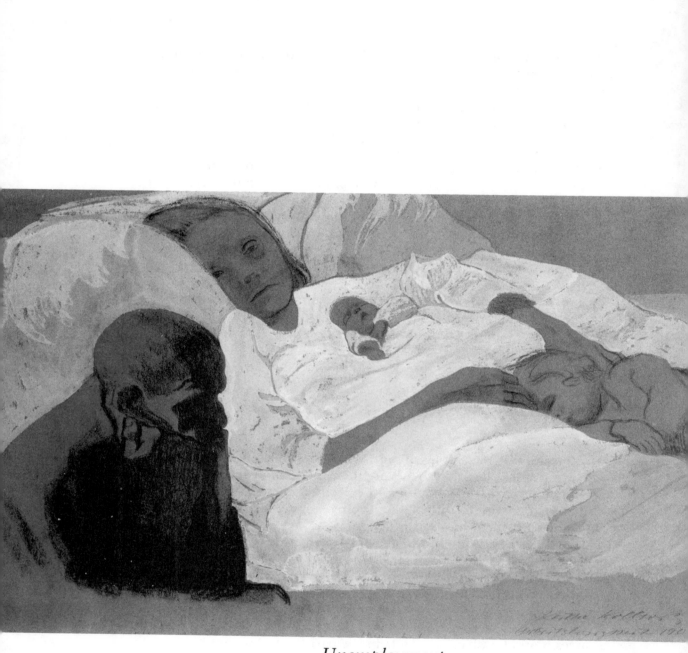

Unemployment

160

EIGHT

Services and Social Action

COMBINING SOCIAL ACTION WITH SERVICES

The Rockford Amendment

"A law that tends to discourage charity toward the needy is perverse, and I'm glad we killed it," said congressman George M. O'Brien of Joliet, IL, after Congress passed the Rockford Amendment to the Social Security Act in 1983. His words also expressed the sentiments of parish social ministry volunteers in Aurora, IL, who were instrumental in killing the law that discouraged charity. They run a food bank sponsored by Aurora parishes.

Before the Rockford Amendment became law, poor elderly Supplemental Security Income (SSI) recipients who received food, shelter, or clothing from service groups such as the Aurora Area Interfaith Food Pantry or the Aurora Soup Bowl, faced the possibility of having their monthly check reduced by as much as 40 percent. The Rockford Amendment changed all that. The story of how this amendment came about furnishes a great example of parishioners combining service with action.

The government policy which penalized the poor for accepting food, clothing or shelter from charitable organizations came to the attention of Rockford Catholic Charities parish outreach coordinator, David Hougan, when an official of the Social Security Administration contacted the director of the Aurora Area Interfaith Food Pantry and wanted to know the value of the food it distributed and the names of the S.S.I. recipients who received help. His inquiries suggested that the value of the donated food would be deducted from the S.S.I. recipients' checks. The food pantry is an inter-parish, ecumenical program of parish Christian Service Leadership and some Protestant ministers.

According to Mr. Hougan, the food program had grown progressively thoughout 1982 to the point of assisting over 6,000 individuals a month with a two-day food supply. "The pantry has been exceedingly successful in terms of gaining broad-based parish support," Mr. Hougan says. When the Social Security official asked for the names of the recipients, "the pantry volunteers blew up and refused."

Parishioners, with help from Catholic Charities, immediately went into action. They contacted their legislators. A lawyer from Holy Angels Christian Service Committee investigated the legality and implications of the existing S.S.I. regulation. He found that the government could indeed penalize poor people for accepting charitable donations of food, clothing, and shelter. Mr. Hougan drafted a letter to the diocese's four congressional members and also contacted the National Conference of Catholic Charities Governmental Relations Office and the United States Catholic Conference Social Development Office for assistance. (The food pantry had received a local Campaign for Human Development grant for initial start-up costs).

During this time Congress was reviewing Social Security Bill revisions. "Our documentation of the abuse incurred because of this regulation gave the only solid piece of support to a dying amendment sponsored by Representative (Charles) Rangle (D-N.Y.)," Mr. Hougan said. He hand-delivered letters to the four Illinois Republicans congressmen representing the Rockford diocese, asking that they investigate the situation and offer some solutions. Congressman O'Brien lobbied for support of the Rangel provision. It became part of the new Social Security Bill and the amendment was extended for three more years in 1984.

"It's a beautiful story," said Mi Loran, coordinator of Christian Service Ministry at Holy Angels parish in Aurora. "It shows church people moving though channels all the way to the top to speak for the poor and do something concrete."

"This example demonstrates how we attempt to inter-relate our works of charity and the works of justice," said Mr. Hougan. "The people who were close to the poor in Aurora saw very easily how the 'system' was unjust and was oppressing the poor. It was a natural and logical step for us then to encourage those involved in this work of charity to seek a sys-

162

tematic change by legislative advocacy. By our inter-relatedness, the parish with the diocese, the diocese with the national offices, I believe our pressure and presence was not ignorable."

The Rockford experience gained a victory not only for the parishes and Catholic Charities, but it benefitted other charitable groups nationwide as well. The Salvation Army and other shelters and rescue missions had also been targeted to provide information about their services to S.S.I. recipients. Because of the action taken by parish social ministry troops, all charitable groups can now serve the poor without fear that the poor will be penalized. "We actually won a victory for the poor of the United States," Dave Hougan says.

SERVICE/ACTION: DOMINANT CHARITIES MODEL

Combining social action with service is not an isolated incident for Catholic Charities parish social ministry. Social ministry includes both charity and justice. The service/action model realizes the Catholic Charities model par excellence. As far back as a decade ago in a 1976 study, Sister Mary Vincentia Joseph and Sister Ann Patrick Conrad clearly found that the combined service/action model was the predominate Charities parish social ministry model. Their report states:

The largest proportion of respondents, or 80.56%, reported both service and action programs. . . .These data clearly support the literature on parish-based programs which claim that there is a dynamic interaction and interdependence between service and action efforts. Despite tensions between the two program models discussed in social work and other literature, these agency-affiliated programs would seem to have achieved an integration of both types of activities. (Joseph and Conrad, *National Trends in Parish Social Ministry: A Study of Parish Programs Affiliated With Catholic Charities Agencies*, p. 15).

The authors further state:

In view of the integrated service and action approach of most parish outreach programs, it was interesting to look at the thrust of the Charities agency in this regard. Thirty agencies (83.33%) engaged in social action and/or community action activities whereas six (16.67%) reported direct service functions only. This would seem to verify the experience of many agency personnel that social action functions are integral to the provision of social services.

The current situation has not changed. Social action combined with service remains the dominant Catholic Charities parish social ministry model. Indeed, the 1983 *Annual Survey* of the National Conference of Catholic Charities shows that almost 80 percent of the reporting Catholic Charities *agencies* combine social action and/or convening functions along with service. And almost 60 percent of the agency parish social ministry programs and 70 percent of agency-affiliated parish social ministry efforts combine services and social action and/or convening efforts. **Catholic Charities conducted well over 1000 parish convenings**

involving almost 31,000 parishioners, making Charities one of the major Church institutions impacting on parish life. "Clearly, the combined service and action direction is our model," says Tara Markey, parish social ministry director, Kansas City, KS Catholic Charities.

SERVICE AND ACTION IN THE PARISH DEVELOPMENT PROCESS

Combining services and social action in parish social ministry may require special efforts. Sometimes parishes develop two separate components in their social ministry, one for services and another for action and they may or may not relate to each other. In recent years, some Charities agencies have utilized a *specific* process, often called the parish development process (sometimes also referred to as a community-building process), which allows for the development of both action and services in one social ministry effort.

Although *all* parish social ministry should aim toward the building of the parish community, this designated community-building process *explicitly* and *self-consciously* sets as its main goal the development of the community. Service and action become the means toward that end. **Emphasis centers on involving all members of the parish in social ministry with the prime objective to create community. Services and action develop as by-products of the process of building the community, rather than as the primary goal**. However, in practice, this difference lies more in emphasis than effect.

The primary service consists of the enhancement of the community itself, the self-realization of the parish as a people of God. Catholic Charities' role in promoting this ministry is very appropriate, for Charities' essential purpose revolves around the expression of the Church as the people of God.

On another level, parish social ministry which emphasizes building community provides, perhaps, the most valuable service of all, especially in this age of individualization where community often remains a lost value. (A survey sent by Salt Lake City Catholic Charities to 12 parishes indicated that their number one concern was greater communication among parishioners and parish/community spirit). ("Parish outreach continues growth in Charities Movement," *Charities Outreach, Review,* No. 11, p. 7).

The parish development process received considerable attention in parish clusters in the San Antonio archdiocese more than 15 years ago. Several Catholic Charities agencies (notably those in the dioceses of Oakland, San Francisco, Mobile, Jacksonville, Alexandria-Shreveport, and Washington, D.C., among others) have since introduced the community-building model with some modifications.* The process deserves attention here because of the widespread acceptance of this model of parish social ministry within the Catholic Charities Movement and because of its embodiment of many of the principles of parish social ministry discussed earlier.

The basic tenets of the formalized community-building process provide that the Christian community reflects and acts on its life experiences in the context of Gospel values. As an integral aspect of the local Christian community, social ministry relates to parish liturgical and teaching functions in an essential way. Social ministry is not relegated to a few social activists. Social ministry becomes part and parcel of the entire worshipping community's activity.

Service and action for justice offer a means to renew parish vitality. At the same time, prayer and reflection provide sustenance to all social ministry activities. Lay leadership receives emphasis. Parishioners create authentic community bonds based on common hopes, values, needs, and responses that are openly acknowledged and shared. (*To Build Community: A Values Process for Parish Outreach*, slide show, NCCC).

The process to create community is deliberate. It creates an identity within the parish and subsequently reaches out into the larger community where transformation and humanizing continue.

Steps of the process include:

1. **Listening**, beginning with the pastor and parish leaders, to what the parish envisions for itself as a parish.
2. **Formation of a parish development team** (a core group) which reflects upon its experiences and the gospel message, and also establishes a vision of parish life. The core group members become apostles, bringing in other parishioners to similar group reflections.
3. Involving the whole parish/community (which may include those

---

*For a step-by-step description of this process, refer to the excellent, **Developing the Parish As a Community of Service**, by Brenda Hermann, M.S.B.T. and Loughlan Sofield, S.T., LeJacq Publishing, Inc., 1984).

166

in the parish neighborhood) to **reflect upon the Gospel message**, and their concerns and vision of community life.

4. Development of a group **plan** to act on the concerns surfaced during the community listening period.

5. **Assembling the parish** to give visibility to and prioritize its concerns and to establish action committees to act on these. This step also includes celebration and liturgy.

6. Formation of **action committees** to carry out the mandates of the parish assembly.

7. **Networking** with other parishes, groups, or organizations on issues of mutual concern. (Sister Margaret Cafferty, "Issues That Emerge from a Special Values-based Parish Development Process," presentation at NCCC Annual Meeting, Sept. 22, 1980, Rochester, NY).

This is the nutshell version of the process which takes minimally about a year to the time of the parish assembly. Many of these steps were included in the parish social ministry principles discussed earlier.

Parishes that have experienced the community-development process find bonds between parishioners strengthened, for they are based in the realities of the community's life experiences, which, in turn, are reflected in the liturgy and educational functions of the parish.

Parish Development at St. Mark's, Richmond, CA

Marge Harrak, co-director of the Parish Outreach Program, Oakland Catholic Charities, explained the application of the community development process at St. Mark's parish. She met with the pastor, Father Joe Farias, described the process to him and listened as he explained his expectations for the parish. "The kinds of things the pastor wanted included leadership development, parishioner participation in parish life, and people to take responsibility," she said. Other major concerns of the pastor included establishment of a parish council; a more solid parish identity (as the parish seemed split into English-speaking and Spanish-speaking groups); and improvement of neighborhood conditions, especially housing.

Father Farias gave Ms. Harrak a list of parish leaders and she interviewed 25 of them individually to get their sense of the parish and to explain the steps of the parish development process.

She scheduled a meeting with the 25 leaders and others at which time they briefly went through the steps of the process, including the timetable and their role in interviewing other parishioners. Since the parish did not have a current census, the core group established a list made up of families registered in CCD and other parish activities. About 40 parishioners agreed to conduct interviews with other parishioners to elicit their concerns. As the people on these lists were interviewed, they were asked to give names of other parishioners they knew who were not on a list.

Charities conducted bilingual training sessions on how to conduct interviews. Material included how to introduce oneself over the phone and how to do the interview. Before the interviews, the parish held a commission service at the Sunday liturgy which gave the interviewers high visibility. The pastor also held a parish outreach Sunday in which he explained why the parish was embarking on parish outreach and he introduced the parish outreach staff person. An informal reception with coffee and donuts and a question/answer session took place after the liturgy.

The interviewers visited about 200 families. "We try to confine this part of the process to about two months at most," Ms. Harrak said.

After completing the interviews, the team and its volunteer hosts conducted house meetings, located in every geographic area of the parish. The outreach staff trained the hosts prior to the meeting.

"The purpose of the house meeting is to give parishioners an opportunity to talk together about their concerns and to surface other issues," Ms. Harrak stated. "The pastor or other parish staff try to attend each meeting."

During the house meetings, the groups decide about the key issues for presentation at the parish convention. Parishioners then prioritize the problems and write resolutions for small group discussions at the convention. Issues St. Mark's parishioners surfaced included a youth group, good liturgy, bible study for Spanish-speaking parishioners, housing workshops, and youth unemployment.

"The process created a sense of community," Ms. Harrak said. "There is a need for people to get to know each other."

St. Mark's is one of 16 parishes in the Oakland diocese that has initiated the parish development process through Catholic Charities in the last five years. Charities staff intentionally target low/moderate income parishes to participate. One of the difficulties that sometimes develops is that the parish doesn't want the Charities staff person to leave the parish. "They often hire someone to carry on. Charities tries to move to a consulting role," Ms. Harrak said.

The highlight of the process centers on the parish assembly which expresses both a celebration and a focal point for the parish's commitment to action. The assembly is "more of a beginning than an ending," according to Sister Margaret Cafferty who had facilitated the process in the San Francisco diocese.

A Parish Convention at St. Andrew's, Daly City, CA

St. Andrew's, a suburban parish in the San Francisco diocese, held a parish assembly or convention that attracted over 300 parishioners. Committees organized months in advance to facilitate arrangements, registration, resolutions, and implementing. An agenda set times for registration, opening songs, and inspirational readings. The pastor gave a state of the parish address and another priest gave a keynote talk. The business part of the assembly focused on 12 resolutions that parishioners brought to the assembly for passage or rejection. The resolutions touched

169

on topics such as forming an adult scripture group; creating a mothers' support group; developing a committee for community safety, etc. Each resolution contained a statement of need, action, responsibility and cost. Parishioners spoke for or against the resolution at microphones designated "pro" and "against." Following discussion, they voted.

Resolutions the parish assembly passed then were given to an implementation committee which monitored the progress of the newly established groups and reviewed new parish concerns. This committee also hired a parish social minister to coordinate the various activities on a day-to-day basis.

A liturgy, at which the resolutions were presented at the offertory, followed the business part of the assembly and a social hour with wine and cheese closed the day's activities. ("Parish conventions invigorate parish/community," *Parish Outreach Review*, No. 12, pp. 8–10).

Parish Development Process Checkpoints

Authority

One of the areas around which problems may arise relates to conflict over authority. Obviously the parish assembly draws extensively on parish resources and requires full support from the pastor who plays a key role, not only during the assembly, but throughout the entire process as all aspects of parish life may be affected by the resolutions which the parishioners pass. The pastor must be thoroughly convinced of the value of this new form of parishioner power. This process demands a high level of maturity on the part of parishioners and pastor. There needs to be a thorough understanding and resolution of the lines of authority before the process begins.

Issues

Another aspect of the process that may require careful observance concerns a tendency toward parochial issues, such as forming a bible study or youth group. Economically comfortable parishes may tend to provide relatively easy services rather than accept more challenging actions for justice. The democratic nature of the process demands vigorous emphasis on Gospel values.

Skilled Personnel

Other possible drawbacks include the lengthy timespan of the process and the need for highly trained and skilled staff. The situations concerning authority and the democratic process require a highly skilled facilitator who possesses sophisticated listening skills, thorough understanding of Gospel values, diplomacy, and an ability to facilitate the parish group to action.

The community-building process offers a challenge to combine service and action. The thoroughness of the process in involving a substantial number of parishioners in social ministry makes it an effective approach. Moreover, the process adheres to most of the parish social ministry principles.

ORGANIZING FOR SERVICE

Pittsburgh

Parish social ministry in the Pittsburgh diocese dates back to 1972, making it one of the oldest diocesan organized parish social ministry programs. Parish social ministry has evolved over the years from primarily a parish referral service toward community-building. Currently 60 parishes participate in Catholic Charities parish social ministry efforts. Charities supports the parishes mainly through training, supervision and support of parish staff and by networking parishes. The parishes hire the social minister. Charities provides an initial four-week training, followed by monthly in-service seminars.

In Pittsburgh, networking with other denominations and organizing parishioners to negotiate with elected officials have been successfully combined with direct services.

Easing the Housing Dilemma:
St. James, Wilkensburg, PA

St. James offers a variety of service ministry programs, such as an information and social program for seniors; transportation and telephone assurance for shut-ins; a "get-well card" program for hospitalized parishioners; a food collection/distribution program; a "paper" bank (collection of products food stamps can't purchase); and a discussion group on parish concerns.

Recently the parish joined forces with 10 Wilkensburg churches to tackle the housing needs in the community. Many parishioners had called Teddie Miller, the parish service minister, about housing needs. The Wilkensburg area has a high number of senior homeowners who are living on limited incomes and who are having difficulty maintaining their homes. The community also has an unusual number of obviously vacant buildings. In January 1985, St. James' pastor, Father Warren Metzler, and Ms. Miller began discussing the community housing problems. At the same time, the Second United Presbyterian Church and the South Avenue United Methodist Church were also discussing and gathering information on community housing needs. The pastor of South Avenue Methodist contacted the Wilkensburg ministerial association to address the issue. From that meeting the 10 churches moved to form the Interfaith Committee on Housing.

"Each of the churches donated $100. St. James donated office space, a telephone, and supervision of the part-time employee," Ms. Miller said. The housing group aims to match those who need shelter with available housing. Three types of housing matches developed:

- help to seniors to maintain their homes by matching them with middle-aged person who will share utilities and rent and also act as a companion. "It's more than a tenant relationship," said Ms. Miller.
- The second group concerns college students who have easy access to the university area in Oakland by matching them with empty apartments.
- Thirdly, the organization tries to match two low income people in an apartment who can share rent since no rental housing is available for the amount allotted through public assistance.

On the drawing board is a concept called "bridge housing" which attempts to place those in rehabilitation centers or emergency shelters in a half-way type residence prior to their finding permanent housing.

Also under consideration is a voucher system for several nights lodging at a local motel for those who need emergency shelter because of a fire or an eviction.

Although the thrust of St. James parish social ministry has been service to the community, it did not hesistate to join in social action by networking with other churches to better meet the community's needs, especially the housing needs of the poor.

Helping Elderly Get Bus Service:
St. Sebastian and St. Teresa Parishes

When a national grocery chain closed one of its stores in Ross Township outside Pittsburgh, it left a great many elderly who lived in a nearby apartment complex without access to a supermarket. Many of these elderly were parishioners of St. Sebastian or St. Teresa parishes, which had social ministry staff trained by Catholic Charities. The two parishes quickly mobilized the elderly residents to ask the township to provide a bus so they could get to a supermarket. There ensued a long struggle between the organized elderly and the township.

A group of seniors from St. Sebastian parish met first with township officials to plead for transportation. Officials promised to investigate ways to fund the transportation. Three months later, nothing had been done. This time 50 seniors from St. Sebastian and St. Teresa churches met again with the township commissioners. At this meeting the township commissioners hedged, asking for more facts before the township could act.

At a third meeting, the township manager told the seniors that the township couldn't afford a bus for them. But the seniors and the parishes social ministers pressed on. "Services in Ross Township are not adequate, and you as elected commissioners have the responsibilitly to address human needs. We're talking about survival. A means to get to doctors and grocery stores," said Sister Carol Sukitz, who was then social minister at St. Sebastian's. (She now heads the diocesan Parish Social Service Program).

The manager agreed to meet with the parish representatives again for further discussion. The commissioners next asked the seniors to present a specific proposal for their bus service. The group quickly surveyed 500 seniors through a form, distributed by the local churches and also placed

in a local newspaper, to learn about their transportation needs. Results revealed that 99 percent of the respondents needed transportation and which areas were most in need. Armed with this information and a proposal for bus service, the group again presented their request for service to the commissioners. After another three months and numerous meetings, the township officials finally approved the proposal and agreed to provide an experimental van for six months for senior citizens. The experiment proved successful, as almost 2000 seniors utilized the bus service during the trial period, and they came back in even greater numbers to meet with township officials to ask for a larger bus. "We should insist, if not demand we get a larger bus," said one township commissioner, a year after the parish-organized seniors made their first request for bus service.

SOCIAL MINISTRIES FORMATION

Training Emphasized in Green Bay

The Green Bay diocese combines service and action components with special emphasis on training. In the late 1970's the diocese established a Social Ministries Formation Program "to prepare leaders for works of charity and justice in their parish and communities." The Social Concerns office conducted an eight-session training program which covered topics such as the church's social mission, models of social ministry, research and planning, organizing skills, advocacy skills, and spirituality for social ministry. ("Parish outreach continues growth in Charities Movement," *Parish Outreach Review*, No. 11, p. 2).

According to Sister Donna Butler of the Social Justice Office, social ministries formation is redeveloped each year. Currently "about 40–50 parishes are doing some ministry, ranging from prison work and peace issues education, to Respect Life."

A new program creating interest is Beyond War, "an educational program to help people change their thinking on how to solve problems—that war is no longer the way," Sr. Butler said. An introductory meeting early in 1985 led to a combined ecumenical meeting, and then an all-day orientation. "People decide where they can take it from there," Sr. Butler said. "Parishioners are trained to give presentations and facilitate meetings. A steering committee acts as consultants, bringing people together

from parishes," she explained. She also noted that in introducing social ministries in the parishes people are service-oriented and it is easier to start from services then continue to social justice. (The diocese is currently reorganizing and developing a core program for all involved in ministry, with the Social Justice Office and the Social Services Office providing special skills training).

EMPOWERMENT TO ACT AND SERVE

St. Alexander's Parish Tackles Unemployment in Villa Park, IL

St. Alexander's parish initiated its social ministry through a year-long empowerment process, assisted by diocesan Parish Social Ministry staff, Mary Ellen Durbin from Catholic Charities and Susan Stolfa from the Social Concerns Office. The parish engaged a social ministry coordinator and established a Christian Service Commission to help link the parishioners with social ministry.

"The parish conducted a systematic, broad-based needs assessment, organized task forces to respond to four prioritized needs, conducted an inventory of parish and community resources, and recruited and trained volunteers for ministries," said Ms. Durbin.

On the issue of unemployment, 40 parishioners volunteered to organize a parish response to that need. They formed a task force and developed direct services and looked into causes of unemployment in the area. Services include a support group, job development, and a job bank.

In addition to providing services, the group studied the issue of unemployment more closely. "The group began to explore the current structure of employment in the area. A key consideration was the imminent closing of the Ovaltine Plant in Villa Park, and action to address the problem of aging factories and companies leaving the area," Ms. Durbin added.

The unemployment issue also led to closer examination of public aid. The parish Christian Service Commission planned a visit to a Public Aid office, presentations from caseworkers and the Public Welfare Coalition, and study of the bishops' Pastoral on the Economy. The Commission also joined with other groups and became active in the Campaign for Family Stability, a statewide lobbying effort to raise monthly grants for public aid recipients.

St. Alexander's illustrates another social ministry approach that combines service with social action.

SUMMARY

The parish and diocesan examples shown here comprise but a small portion of the many parishes engaged in social ministry that combine both direct services and social action. Catholic Charities holds that this dual aspect—charity and justice—offers an ideal expression of social ministry and it provides the means to utilize every parishioner's gifts for the good of the community.

178

Part IV:

Conclusion

Death Cycle: Death in the Water

NINE

Conversion: The Challenge of Social Ministry

send the spirit of adoption
to regenerate the new people
whom the baptismal font brings forth;
so that by the effect of Your power
we may accomplish what we are to do
through our own humble ministry.
Easter Vigil liturgy

This prayer of the blessing of the baptismal water clearly indicates the relationship between our baptismal death and rebirth and the founding of our ministry. The waters of baptism regenerate us, make us adopted children of God, and initiate us into our ministry.

By baptism, with Christ we are buried and born of Spirit and water to a new life, to journey as a pilgrim people toward the Kingdom (as the people of God in the Exodus journeyed through the waters toward a new land).

Social ministry, the ministry of the people, the ministry of mediation, positions us to share in the mysteries of the pain, suffering and death of the Lord as experienced by His brothers and sisters.

Social ministry closely identifies with sacramental life. At the Eucharistic liturgy, we enter into and share in the mystery of Christ's death and suffering. Modern poet Gerard Manley Hopkins poignantly links the myster-

ies of death and suffering with the Eucharist in the poem, "*The Wreck of the Deutschland*," which pays tribute to five Franciscan nuns who drowned while on an exile journey in 1875:

> The frown of his face
> Before me, the hurdle of hell
> Behind, where, where was a, where was a place?
> I whirled out wings that spell
> And fled with a fling of the heart to the heart of the Host.

In the face of death, the Christian flees to the heart of the Host, the place where death, that most profane effect of sin, becomes sacred. The Eucharist and the events of Good Friday express the quintessential mysteries of death and suffering for Christians.

Each of us shares in the mysteries of death and suffering in a special way, which begins with our first death in the waters of baptism and continues sacramentally through the Eucharist, confirmation, and through our ministry.

What distinguishes social *ministry* from social *work*? Although on the practical plane, both may require many similar skills, social ministry is inextricably bound to sacramental life: life renewed through baptism, nourished through the Eucharist and nurtured in confirmation. In a sense, social ministry moves us to die *for* the world.

We "cannot forget the suffering world which until the end of time is the preoccupation of the heart of Christ. . . ." (Gerald Vann, O.P., *The Divine Pity*, p. 18). Father Vann explores the connection between spiritu-

182

ality, or closeness to God, and action, "the doing for one's neighbor," the compulsion to serve.

". . .the love of the world does not make sense apart from the love of God, precisely because it is wholly and entirely an expression of the love of God. . . .it is also a total misunderstanding to suppose that we can work for the world, as Christians, and so become saints, without being identified with Christ." (Vann, pp. 22, 19).

Social ministry presupposes a global spirituality for it is bound to the "suffering world." The modern era presents, in fact, bombards us with panoramic images of death and suffering in daily news reports, literature, and mock entertainment. Death and suffering, common, but unnatural experiences of all humans, remain unfathomable mysteries to daily confront Christians in their ministry.

"Apart from me you can do nothing" (*John 15:5*).

Spirituality leads to action, but action without spirituality, without charity, as St. Paul says, "profits nothing." (*Corinthians 13:3*).

Social ministry invites us to enter into the realm of the Beatitudes, into the world of the blessed. Who are the blessed? Jesus calls blessed those who

- are poor in spirit—carefree stewards of their material and spiritual gifts;
- are meek—zealous to do the work of the Lord;
- mourn—who embrace suffering;
- hunger and thirst after justice—passionately insist that attitudes and actions toward others reflect their human dignity;
- are merciful—generous to the needs of others;
- clean of heart—reverence all things and people;
- peacemakers—bridgemakers—a priestly people—mediators of unity.

Häring, also, in his book, *The Beatitudes*, links individual spirituality and mission. He notes that one cannot serve others except as a person of prayer. We must always return for the nourishment of the sacraments and prayer if we are to care for others.

As a pilgrim people reconciling all things to Christ, we mark our journey with difficulties, often like the Magi in their journey to Christ, who protested:

> This Birth was
> Hard and bitter agony for us, like Death,
> (T. S. Eliot, "*Journey of the Magi*").

183

Hard and sometimes bitter indeed! But the community supports us in our journey. Community, particularly the parish community, offers "a safe place to suffer through our pain," notes Henry Nouwen. Nouwen's community of a safe place does not imply "a cosy kind of community in which we come together and avoid having to deal with the real problems, where we cling together to feel safe because we are all scared together."

His notion of community is of a people "on the move," very much like that of the people of God in the Exodus, and of Eliot's Magi ("worst time of the year for a journey").

The Church "is called to create a space where we are free to face the real struggle, where we are free to face our true pain, where we are free (to use a more theological word) to realize how sinful we are, and therefore a place where we can discover the need for God's grace and mercy." ("the parish. . .a safe place to face our pain, an interview with Henri Nouwen," *Alban Institute Action Information*, January–February 1981).

Parish social ministry enters into sin, pain, suffering, and death in the everyday struggles of our brothers and sisters. Parish social ministry, conceived in the baptismal waters, identifies with the Eucharist Christ who dies so all may have life. Parish social ministry spurs us on our journey, challenges our cosiness, demands a change of heart—an awesome respect in the presence of another—and speaks of a radical transformation within those who minister; in short, it presumes conversion.

At the root of social ministry lies a profound hope, hope that emanates from the promise of the Lord who will say:

184

These are they who have come out of great tribulation. . .They shall neither hunger nor thirst any more. . .and God will wipe away every tear from their eyes. (*Apoc: 7:14*).

That hope, according to Father Thomas Harvey, springs from the prayer of Jesus, who when He was about to die, spoke with the Father: "I have glorified you on earth; I have accomplished the work you have given me to do." (*John 17:4*).

His prayer becomes our prayer—our ministry—a sign of how we are to live our lives. But with what awesome results: to glorify the Father! "The work for us is to bring the world to Christ. When we meet God, we, too, will have on our lips the words of the Lord: 'I have finished the work you have given me to do.'"

References, Sources
and Selected Bibliography

Books

ABBOTT, WALTER, S.J. and JOSEPH GALLAGHER, editors. *The Documents of Vatican II*. New York: Guild Press, 1966.

ALINSKY, SAUL. *Reveille for Radicals*. New York: Random House, 1969.

————. *Rules for Radicals*. New York: Random House, 1972.

COLEMAN, JOHN A.. *An American Strategic Theology*. New York: Paulist Press, 1982.

HÄRING, BERNARD. *The Beatitudes: Their Personal and Social Implications*. St. Paul Publications, Middlegreen, Slough, 1976.

The Holy Bible. New York: Catholic Book Publishing Co., 1957.

KUNICZAK, W.S. *My Name is Million*. New York: Doubleday and Company, 1978.

SOFIELD, LOUGHLAN, S.T. and BRENDA HERMANN, M.S.B.T. *Developing the Parish As a Community of Service*. Le Jacq Publishing Co., 1984.

VANN, GERALD, O.P. *The Divine Pity*. New York: Sheed and Ward, Image Books edition, 1961.

WHITEHEAD, EVELYN E., ed. *The Parish In Community and Ministry*. New York: Paulist Press, 1978.

WILLIAMS, OSCAR, ed. *Immortal Poems of the English Language*. New York: Washington Square Press, Inc., 1966.

Booklets, Periodicals and Papers

A Code of Ethics. Washington, D.C.: National Conference of Catholic Charities, 1984.

Agenda for Action 1978 Policy Statement. (Parish/Community Social Ministry). Washington, D.C.: National Conference of Catholic Charities.

BIERSBACH, RAY. "Parish Social Ministry: A Theological Statement." Unpublished paper. January 31, 1984.

BISHOPS' SYNOD. "Justice in the World." Washington, D.C.: United States Catholic Conference, 1971.

DOWNING, JOHN. "Elderly Ask Ross for Shopping Lift." *Pittsburgh Press*, 31 October 1979, p. 18.

GILMARTIN, JOHN. *A Parish Social Ministry in the Diocese of Rockville Centre: Parish Outreach*. Rockville Centre, NY: Catholic Charities, 1983.

Guidelines Organization/Personnel. Washington, D.C.: National Conference of Catholic Charities, 1985.

JOHN PAUL II. *Redemptor Hominis*. Papal Encyclical, March 15, 1979.

JOSEPH, SISTER MARY VINCENTIA and SISTER ANN PATRICK CONRAD. *National Trends in Parish Social Ministry: A Study of Parish Programs Affiliated with Catholic Charities Agencies*. Washington, D.C.: National Conference of Catholic Charities, 1977.

HARVEY, THOMAS J.. "The Church: Called to Serve." *Charities USA*, March 1983.
——————. "Maintaining Catholic Identity in a Pluralistic Society." *Hospital Progress*, January 1983, pp. 48–53.

"The Houmas in Jefferson Parish." *Parishes in ACCtion*, Vol. 5, No. 2, April 1985. Newsletter published by Associated Catholic Charities of New Orleans.

McCARTHY, SHEILA. "How to start a parish outreach project: An organizer's approach." *Parish Outreach Review*, No. 8, Summer 1978, pp. 2–3. Quarterly news magazine of the National Conference of Catholic Charities Parish Outreach Project.

MAINELLI, VINCENT P. *The Pastor's Role as Servant Leader in Parish Social Ministry*. Washington, D.C.: National Conference of Catholic Charities, 1977.

MILLER, JULIAN J., S.T.L. "Towards a Theology of Parish Social Ministry: A Working Paper." Paper presented at the NCCC Parish Social Ministry Task Force Eastern Regional Convening, May 1 and 2, 1984.

"Models for Parish Outreach." Department of Social Affairs, Diocese of Savannah.

MOWBRAY, JEAN. "Theological Reflections." Paper presented at NCCC Parish Social Ministry Task Force Midwest Regional Convening, April 24, 1984.

MYOTT, TOM. "Parish Social Ministry: A Theological Statement." Unpublished Paper, St. Paul, MN: May 27, 1984.

NCCC Annual Survey 1983. Washington, D.C.: National Conference of Catholic Charities, November 1984.

"the parish . . . a safe place to face our pain, an interview with Henri Nouwen." *Alban Institute Action Information*, January–February 1981, The Alban Institute, Inc., Washington, D.C.

"Parish outreach continues growth in Charities Movement." *Parish Outreach Review*, No. 11, Fall 1979, pp. 1–2.

Parish Outreach Quarterly, Fall 1983. New Hampshire Catholic Charities newsletter.

"Parish Social Ministry." Unpublished paper. Denver Catholic Charities and Community Services, Inc. January 29, 1983.

"Parish social ministry is basis for Charities renewal Committee states." *Parish Outreach Review*, No. 10, Spring 1979, p. 1. Report on NCCC Parish/Community Social Ministry Committee statement which gives an early definition of parish social ministry and its incorporation into the Charities Movement.

Parish Social Ministry Resource Booklet. Diocesan Human Relations Services, Waterville, Maine. Brief examples of parish social ministries.

Parish Social Ministry Resource Handbook. Catholic Family Service, Inc. Lubbock, Texas.

PEELER, ALEXANDRA. "Parish conventions invigorate parish/community," *Parish Outreach Review*, No. 12, Winter 1979–80, pp. 8–10.

————. "Parish Social Ministry as the Primary Focus for the Agency," *Parish Outreach Review*, No. 18, Spring 1982, pp. 1–5.

————. "Agency is resource for community development." *Parish Rural Review*, No. 4, Spring 1982, pp. 1–2.

"Ross approves plan for free rides for senior citizens." *North Hills News Record*, 12 June 1980. Pittsburgh suburban weekly describes seniors' fight for transportation.

"Ross doesn't want to adopt 'son of PAT' for senior citizens." *North Hills News Record*, 30 November 1979, p. D–4.

SELLNER, EDWARD C. "Discernment of Vocation for Pastoral Ministry." *Spirituality Today*, Spring 1985, pp. 47–56.

"Senior citizens and Ross to extend its van service." *North Hills News Record*, 11 November 1980.

Seven Great Encyclicals. Glen Rock, N.J.: Paulist Press, 1963.

TWOOMEY, GERALD S. "Liturgy and Social Justice." *Passage*. Amityville, NY: Catholic Charities/Parish Outreach of the Diocese of Rockville Centre.

Toward a Renewed Catholic Charities Movement. Washington, D.C.: National Conference of Catholic Charities, 1972. The "Cadre" self-study which solidified the Charities Movement road to renewal.

U.S. Bishops. "Called and Gifted: Catholic Laity, 1980." *Origins*, Vol. 10, No. 24, 27 November 1980.

Volunteer Training Manual. Chicago Parish/Community Services, Catholic Charities of the Archdiocese of Chicago. A wealth of "how-to" material.

WADE, CHET. "Bus for elderly: Bigger, better." *Post-Gazette North*, 20 November 1980.

Interviews, Speeches, Presentations, Discussions, Letters

BAKER, BOB, Portland, OR. Telephone interview by Alexandra Peeler, August 1984.

BUTLER, DONNA, Green Bay, WI. Telephone interview by Alexandra Peeler, March 6, 1985.

BAUDOUIN, MARY, New Orleans, LA. Telephone interview by Alexandra Peeler, May 3, 1985.

_____. Letters to Alexandra Peeler, July 20, 1984; August 13, 1984.

BRACAMONTE, REY, El Centro, CA. Telephone interview by Alexandra Peeler, March 18, 1985.

CAFFERTY, MARGARET. Training sessions. San Francisco, CA: November 13–19, 1979.

_____. Training sessions. Washington, D.C.: January 7–9, 1980.

_____. "Issues that Emerge from a Special Values-based Parish Development Process, Part I." Presentation at NCCC Annual Meeting, Rochester, NY, September 22, 1980.

CREEDON, GERARD. Alexandria, VA. Telephone interview by Alexandra Peeler, January 1985.

DELLA MONICA, PETER, Brooklyn, NY. Telephone interview by Alexandra Peeler, May 14, 1985.

DE STEFANO, THOMAS, interviewed by Alexandra Peeler, Brooklyn, NY, February 4, 1977. Telephone interview, April 1985.

_____. Letters to Rosemary Winder Strange, March 27, 1985; April 15, 1985.

DOLAN, FRANCIS, Philadelphia, PA. Telephone interviews by Alexandra Peeler, May 3, 1985; May 24, 1985.

DURBIN, MARY ELLEN, Lockport, IL. Letter to Alexandra Peeler, May 4, 1985.

ERNST, JEROME, Washington, D.C. Letter to Rosemary Winder Strange, July 17, 1985.

FINERAN, SHIRLEY, Chicago, IL. Telephone interview by Alexandra Peeler, April, May 1985.

_____. Letter to Alexandra Peeler, August 16, 1984.

GILMARTIN, JOHN. Discussion at NCCC Parish Social Ministry Task Force Meeting, Washington, D.C., May 31–June 1, 1984.

_____. Letter to Alexandra Peeler, May 9, 1985.

GRAYKOSKI, JOHN, Stockton, CA. Telephone interview by Alexandra Peeler, March 1985.

JOHN PAUL II. *Opening Address at Celam*, January 28, 1979.

_____. *Papal Talk at Limerick*, Ireland, October 1, 1979.

_____. *Homily at Yankee Stadium*, October 2, 1979.

_____. *The Important Roles of the Laity*. Homily at Toledo, Spain, November 4, 1983.

HARRAK, MARGE, Oakland, CA. Telephone interview by Alexandra Peeler, May 3, 1985.

HARTMANN, MARIA MERCEDES. Conversation with Rosemary Winder Strange, April 1985.

HAY, STEVE, Lubbock, TX. Telephone interview by Alexandra Peeler, March 1985.

HERMANN, BRENDA, Alexandria, LA. Telephone interview by Alexandra Peeler, August 26, 1985.

————. Letter to Alexandra Peeler, May 21, 1985.

HOLT, STAN. "Issues that Emerge from a Special Values-Based Parish Development Process, Part III." Presentation at NCCC Annual Meeting, Rochester, NY, September 23, 1981.

HOUGAN, DAVID, Rockford, IL. Letter to Alexandra Peeler, October 26, 1984.

LEAMING-ELMER, DON, Washington, D.C. Interview by Alexandra Peeler, November 22, 1978.

LEE, TONY, Seattle, WA. Telephone interview by Alexandra Peeler, May 2, 1985.

LONG, BETH, Alexandria, VA. Telephone interviews by Alexandra Peeler, January and May 1985; and with Rosemary Winder Strange, May 1985.

McGEADY, ROSE, interviewed by Alexandra Peeler, Brooklyn, NY, February 4, 1977.

MARKEY, TARA, Kansas City, KS. Telephone interview by Alexandra Peeler, March 4, 1985.

MILLER, TEDDIE, Wilkensburg, PA. Telephone interview by Alexandra Peeler, May 14, 1985.

National Conference of Catholic Charities Parish Social Ministry Task Force Meeting. Washington, D.C.: May 31–June 1, 1984.

National Conference of Catholic Charities Parish Social Ministry Task Force Convenings: Chicago, IL, Midwest Meeting, April 27, 1984; Denver, CO, Western Meeting, April 28, 1984; Long Island, NY, Eastern Meeting, May 1–2, 1984; Dallas, TX, Southern Meeting, May 6–8, 1984.

OPALACH, JUDY, Cleveland, OH. Telephone interview by Alexandra Peeler, May 7, 1985.

PIUS XII. Christmas Message, 1948.

SMITH, ROLLAND, Honolulu, HI. Telephone interview by Alexandra Peeler, May 1, 1985.

SULLIVAN, BISHOP JOSEPH. "Parish Outreach: most hopeful sign in Charities." Excerpts from an informal talk. *Parish Outreach Review*, No. 16, Summer 1981, p. 3.

SHANNON, RICHARD, Manchester, NH. Letters to Alexandra Peeler, February 20, 1985 and April 9, 1985.

SUKITZ, CAROL, Pittsburgh, PA. Telephone interview by Alexandra Peeler, May 4, 1985.

UJVEGI, PETER. Interviewed by Alexandra Peeler, Toledo, OH., March 18, 1977.

VERA, JOSEFINA, Plainview, TX. Telephone interview by Alexandra Peeler, May 24, 1985.

WALSH, AUSTIN, S.T. "Spirituality for Social Ministry." Talk given at Catholic Charities Social Ministry Fair, New Orleans, LA., May 7, 1983.

WARD, PETER. Interviewed by Alexandra Peeler, Bloomingdale, N.Y., October 11, 1980.

ZIRBES, SISTER MARY, Minneapolis, MN. Audio tape sent to Alexandra Peeler, August 8, 1984.

————. Letters to Alexandra Peeler, May 27, 1985; May 28, 1985.

Audiovisuals

NATIONAL FILM BOARD OF CANADA. *Organizing for Power; the Alinsky Approach.* Series of motion picture films, 1968.

PEELER, ALEXANDRA. *To Build Community: A Values Process for Parish Outreach.* 35 mm slide show produced for NCCC Parish Outreach Project, 1980.

PEELER PRODUCTIONS. *The Ethnic Response: Parish/Neighborhood Survival.* 16 mm film, 1978.

_____. *Parish Outreach: Building Community Through Service and Action.* 35 mm slide show produced for NCCC Parish Outreach Project, 1977.

Photographs

The illustrations introducing each chapter are works by KATHE KOLLWITZ, reproduced with permission from THE NATIONAL GALLERY of Art, Washington, D.C. ROSENWALD COLLECTION

p. 3   *Self-portrait* (B-13, 939)

p. 25   *The Homeless* (1944.8.2)

p. 49   *Working Woman with Sleeping Child* (B-7, 759)

p. 75   *The Shelter* (B-7, 765)

p. 89   *Sitting Woman* (1954.12.32)

p. 125   *Woman Weeping* (1943.3.5221)

p. 145   *Bread* (B-7, 771)

p. 161   *Unemployment* (1943.3.5218)

p. 181   *Death Cycle: Death in the Water* (B-7, 743)

Photographs courtesy of:

CATHOLIC CHARITIES OF THE ARCHDIOCESE OF ST. PAUL AND MINNEAPOLIS: pp. 100, 102, 138.

CATHOLIC CHARITIES OF THE ARCHDIOCESE OF ST. PAUL AND MINNEAPOLIS AND ST. JEROME parish: pp. 28, 31, 98.

CATHOLIC CHARITIES OF THE ARCHDIOCESE OF ST. PAUL AND MINNEAPOLIS AND RESURRECTION parish: pp. 36, 82.

CATHOLIC CHARITIES OF THE ARCHDIOCESE OF ST. PAUL AND MINNEAPOLIS AND ST. PETER'S parish: p. 168.

CATHOLIC CHARITIES AND COMMUNITY SERVICES, INC. Denver, CO: pp. 14, 178.

CATHOLIC CHARITIES INC. OF THE DIOCESE OF TULSA: p. 63.

DIOCESAN HEALTH AND SOCIAL SERVICES, Albany, NY: p. 22.

PARISH COMMUNITY SERVICES, CATHOLIC CHARITIES OF THE ARCHDIOCESE OF CHICAGO: pp. 23, 62, 153.